In Their Own Words: Research on Refugee Women's Experiences

Dr Lin Armstrong

First Edition

First published in Great Britain in 2023

Copyright © 2023 Dr Lin Armstrong

All rights reserved.

ISBN: 9798848949117

Edited by Sue Sampson
Cover design by Michael Robinson-Hart

Disclaimer
The content and findings presented in this book are based on real-life experiences and research. The names and identifying details of individuals mentioned in this book have been altered to protect their privacy and maintain confidentiality. This modification aims to ensure that no personal or sensitive information is disclosed and that the privacy rights of all individuals involved are respected.

FOREWARD

Foreward from Sue Sampson – CEO and founder of Carriers of Hope, Coventry.
I am pleased to be writing in support of this book which is both a "How To" aid to all carrying out research with asylum seekers and refugees, especially students in Higher Education; and important messages for us all, coming from the research, in refugees' own voices. It focuses on best practice methods of including and working with refugees and those who are seeking asylum. Research done well is empowering and can be the first step to yet more active involvement in its outcomes. In this book you will read of the first-hand experience of the women that Dr Lin Armstrong has been working with over the past 6 years. She has a gift for getting the women to speak openly and share their experience.

Dr Lin demonstrates through a series of case studies that engagement and giving a "voice" to refugees within the research process have benefits at various levels. It produces much more accurate research data and develops the skills and confidence of the participants in the research groups.

The research reports show, sadly, that many questions are still to be answered about how we can all become fairer, more ethical and humane to these particular target groups, who are among the poorest of the poor in our society.

FOREWARD II

Foreward from Will Armstrong.
Lin Armstrong, my mother, Is the most thoughtful, kind and passionate person I know. She has spent her life deliberately in roles which allowed her to help others, in particular families and children.
She's gone from working as a nursery nurse to a social work manager, to a senior lecturer in child development. She completed a PhD while working full time and raising 3 children and remains an inspiration for me, and many others who have had the good fortune to know her.
Now, in retirement, she volunteers her time and experience to empower refugees and asylum seekers living in poverty.
She supports the education of children who have seen harsher shades of reality than most adults.
She helps source food and provide a safe space and secure footing from which to grow. All in the community she grew up in as a child, Hillfields in Coventry, as an Irish immigrant.
Thanks for taking the time to read this.

CONTENTS

1 Introduction 1

2 Writing an Opinion Piece 3

3 Using Artificial Intelligence 7

4 Research Methodology 11

5 Creating a survey for use with refugee women 14

6 Writing up the results of the maternity research 18

7 Presenting One's Findings by way of a Research Paper – "What refugee women say about the Importance of Singing" 26

8 Presenting One's Findings – Creating an oral presentation using research methods 32

9 Preparing a Synopsis 40

10 Educating Fatima and Her Sisters 42

11 Writing Reflective Accounts 46

12 A systematic review of the literature (secondary research) 54

13 Write a Rationale For Research 61

14 A Boolean Search for Literature 68

15 Acknowledging the Researcher's Lens - Navigating Bias in Scientific Inquiry 74

16 Ethnography as a Choice of Method - Exploring the Dynamics of Researching Lived Experiences 76

17 Research planning and supervision 80

18 Citizens social research 90

19 Last Word 126

References 127

1 INTRODUCTION

I'm excited to write this book in the first person, as I'll share my experiences and insights throughout. My passion for innovative teaching and learning practices has always been fuelled by my desire to help those easily excluded from education, particularly women and children.

I've previously written books on creating fairness for women returning to university and teaching people with dyslexia. These books are available on Amazon, and I'm proud to have shared my knowledge and expertise with a broader audience.

With this new book, I'm eager to continue sharing my experience and insights and to inspire others to create a more inclusive and equitable education system. Everyone should have access to education, regardless of gender, ethnicity, or socio-economic status.

Through this book, I hope to provide practical advice and guidance for others working in similar contexts and encourage them to share innovative teaching and learning practices that can help break down barriers to education.

Who is this book aimed at, and why would people want to read this work? I had in mind two specific groups when writing this book:

Group 1. Tutors in Higher Education who are encouraging their students to carry out direct research with refugees. The innovation of working with refugees will benefit institutional development, programme development and professional development of the tutors and students. However, lacking familiarity with the group may deter academics from seeking research in this field. The aspects in this book about women and children's lives will increase effective practice and introduce variety to the lectures and research projects set by tutors.

Group 2. College and University students at Levels 3, 4 and 5, where learning modules require demonstrating authentic case studies. However, gaining authenticity when conducting research with an unknown group is difficult. Therefore, I recommend that students participate somehow with people who could help to do the research, the refugees themselves. A lived experience affects the student and practitioner, so I urge inclusive research or ethnography by volunteering to work with a charity or night shelter.

Listening to the diverse "truths" as refugees see them will lead to diversity in the dialogue about children and their families, thus transforming the students and tutor who hope to create equality in their work.

How This Book Came About

The notion that students need to be taught in a way to suit their situation is familiar to educators. Teaching and collaborative learning are much more effective and enjoyable when the activities are culturally appropriate and meaningful to the student. The lack of materials *and studies concerning minority groups, refugees and asylum seekers has led to the main objectives of this book which are.

1. To uncover women and their children's private lives and educational barriers. I hope others will research and add their voice to challenge the inequalities and improve educational outcomes for refugees and asylum seekers.
2. To present theories, models, concepts, and paradigms educators consider or need to learn about when evaluating their teaching practice with marginalised groups, especially refugees and asylum seekers.
3. Present strategies and methods for real-life research that may be useful to the new researcher.

*Similar books are unavailable except those listed here; Temple, B. and Moran, R. eds., 2006. Doing research with refugees: Issues and guidelines. Policy Press.

As I reflect on my journey, spanning over five decades of working with children and families, I am humbled by the lessons I have learned. From my early days in social services to my current work in educational organisations, I have witnessed first-hand the impact of using power and genuine empathy in supporting those in need.

My experiences have taught me that actual change and progress come from a deep understanding of the needs and desires of the people we serve. It is not enough to listen to their voices; we must empower them to control their lives and shape their futures.

As I embarked on a new career chapter, I joined the charity in 2018; I am filled with a renewed sense of purpose. I am eager to use my expertise and experience to amplify the voices of refugees and asylum seekers, helping them navigate the challenges they face and achieve their full potential.

Through my research and writing, I aim to inspire others to embrace the power of empathy and understanding in their work. Doing so can build stronger, more resilient communities that uplift and support one another, regardless of background or circumstance.

I am grateful for the opportunity to share my story and the stories of those I have worked with over the years. Let us strive for a world that values compassion, equity, and justice.

The Organisation of the Book Chapters

Each chapter focuses on the relationship between academic theory and practice in the context of academic writing. This book explores how educational theory can inform and shape academic writing practice and how academic writing practice can contribute to and challenge literary theory.

The first section of the chapter provides a theoretical overview of academic writing. It discusses the purpose of academic writing, the conventions, and the standards of academic writing. The sections also explore the relationship between academic writing and critical thinking, highlighting the importance of evidence-based argumentation and the need to engage with multiple perspectives.

The second section of each chapter presents a series of practice-based examples that demonstrate how academic theory can be applied in practice. The illustrations are drawn from my research. Each instance presents a specific case study or project, highlighting how the academic approach was used to inform and shape the research process and the writing of the final report or paper.

A last section is the research the asylum seekers carried out with their companions in a refuge for mothers and babies. This is called social research .

The book concludes by reflecting on the relationship between academic theory and practice in academic writing. It argues that theory and practice are intimately connected, and that educational writing practice can contribute to and challenge literary theory. By critically engaging with academic theory and applying it in practice, academic writing can be used to generate new knowledge and advance the field.

2 WRITING AN OPINION PIECE

In academic work, a written opinion piece is a form of scholarly writing that presents an author's subjective viewpoint or perspective on a particular topic or issue. Unlike more objective forms of academic writing, such as research papers or literature reviews, opinion pieces primarily focus on expressing personal opinions, arguments, and interpretations.

Opinion pieces are typically found in newspapers, magazines, or online platforms that allow authors to express their thoughts on current events, social issues, politics, or other relevant subjects. However, in the context of academic work, opinion pieces may also be written and published within scholarly journals, particularly in fields where subjective analysis and critical evaluation are valued, such as philosophy, cultural studies, or certain branches of social sciences This is just like the other chapters, is split into theory and practice; the first section is the theory about writing an opinion piece. The second section is an opinion piece about teaching academic writing skills to students. Prompts for an academic opinion piece. (AI 2023)

When writing an opinion piece for an academic publication is essential to follow specific rules and guidelines to ensure that your work is well-received by readers and contributes to the overall quality and credibility of the book rest.

1. *Clearly state your opinion:* It is essential to voice your opinion at the outset of your piece. This will help readers understand the perspective from which you are writing.
2. *Use credible sources:* While personal opinions are based on your thoughts and experiences, use credible sources to support your claims. This will lend credibility to your argument and help convince readers of the validity of your opinion.
3. *Consider opposing views:* It is essential to consider opposing viewpoints and address potential counterarguments in your piece. This will demonstrate that you have thought critically about your opinion and are open to considering other perspectives.
4. *Use evidence:* Besides using credible sources, it is important to use evidence to support your claims. This may include statistics, anecdotes, or other evidence that illustrate your point.
5. *Write clearly and concisely*: It is important to write clearly and concisely to make your point effectively. This will help readers understand your perspective and engage with your argument.
6. *Avoid personal attacks*: While it is important to express your opinion, it is also essential to do so respectfully and professionally. Avoid personal attacks or derogatory language that could detract from the overall quality of your piece.
7. *Review and revise*: Finally, reviewing and editing your piece before submitting it for publication is essential. This will help ensure that your writing is clear, concise, and well-supported and that your opinion is presented compellingly.

An Opinion Piece on Teaching Academic Writing Skills to Students

Whenever academics discuss their marking duties, they might comment negatively on the academic tone and lack of referencing in the student's work, according to Kennedy et al. (2017) Significantly, only some students gain a high grade at the beginning of the course, which academic staff accepts as a problem with the students. Staff cite issues such as the recruitment to the course needing to be set higher. 'The students should have taken on board their study skills course." "The students all copied each other." "Students produce no original reading or writing; "students are just patchworking the lecture notes together". Dong (1996) expanded on the notion that academics do not teach academic writing skills robustly, but tutors do not recognise this.

Contemporary university modules are recorded and presented online to give any day; any time offered to students. Enabling the new student to learn how to transform their writing from a pass grade (descriptive type of work) to better means the tutors must focus on a good experience of finding information and learning how to put it all together. This is one of the joys of being a tutor. Tayler (2023) writes about the transition between level 3 and level 4 and makes a good case for becoming an independent and autonomous student.

Yet more and more students have to fear their learning by getting others to write it for them or plagiarising through internet materials. This is a cry for help, not a lazy way to gain a relevant degree, and intervention will reduce the need to plagiarise (Obeid and Hill, 2017.)

Strategic planning in universities is led by the economics of less and less time spent on modules. Ashworth (1997) suggests that university strategic planning is driven by economic considerations, leading to a decrease in the time allocated to modules or courses. This implies that universities may prioritise efficiency and cost-effectiveness in their planning processes at the expense of providing comprehensive and in-depth learning experiences through modules.

Student writing often needs improvement, and tutors must improve their strategies to enable students to write. A lack of contact with the tutor is often cited as a problem in knowing how the writing is going.

At the start and end of degrees, students' modules still score bare passes; therefore, academic writing and thinking learning did not occur. This "learning to write" skill will be needed in all situations after the degree. Many students never come to learn about their voice and, therefore, will not manage to change their identity to become a writer, an academic who can state their opinions in writing papers or books. This graduate attribute can add to the discourse in the world.

Literacy is developed in our own culture, and the tutor in university should strive to learn about the cultures operating in their classrooms. Primary socialisation and the growth of literacies begin in the family. The spoken language is developed to read and write as a young child. Then the type of literacy required in academia is the ability to access texts and papers and interpret them. Formally learning about dealing with specialised writing in the discipline chosen is often the first gap in a student's knowledge. A second-year foundation degree student in one of the classes asked, "What paper do you keep referring to?"

The lecture must include basic questions such as "Where does research come from?" to help a student contextualise the reading. It also helps if a tutor can critically evaluate the reading in class.

Social distance and diversity among students are sometimes not considered in a traditional university. The reading for the programmes is posted onto the course module, and students must learn how to use the platforms and interfaces quickly. At the end of their course, many still need to know how to search in the university library or locate specific support for their reflections on the discipline. No wonder new knowledge is hard to assimilate for new students. Many students think it would be safer to get hold of a previous student's assignment and patchwork it. Plagiarism can be a direct response to poor teaching of information literacy skills, according to Barbazon (2016),

The degree student should learn theory and current thinking about their discipline, yet there needs to be formal teaching on how to do this. For example, a set of reference cards need to be organised and memorised in a sensible order, and a student needs to be taught how to do this. Awareness of critical reflective literature will lead to more logical academic activity after the degree. Learning how to learn and use reading is a skill that should be taught.

Another issue is the sharing and commentary on literacy to propel the student's critical examination of what they read. Moving through papers with a critical and explicit analysis of what the group is reading can be done at home and returned to the group. Encoding and decoding with other students and academic staff will shape the behaviour of selecting literature from the search engine and putting it together to make an argument. The academic assignment will receive a lower grade if a step in digital literacy needs to be understood. More importantly, the text read and discussed is set in a context that immediately becomes memorable and more easily reflected upon. Translation of specialised vocabulary and clear memory of how it came about leads the student to the ability to use the language necessary in public debates and to be able to disseminate their ideas across disciplines. A tutor is responsible for this leadership process but needs more time to teach content.

Content is a choice for tutors, and often they find lots of 'reading to add to the course modules on a Virtual learning platform such as Moodle/blackboard/Kajabi.

Feedback from students states that the vague descriptors of the reading content on the VLP could be more helpful to learners new to the discipline. This is when students turn to easier reads such as magazine articles. Tutors need their skills developing to teach how to access specialised literacies, and they need to recognise and provide various levels of reading. Academic research papers can be difficult to decode because they are levelled at a different audiences.

The students are often instructed to read, listen to a podcast, or view a piece of media at home. Their engagement with literacies is considered a way to help everyone engage with specialist knowledge. Multi-modal options and alternatives respect students' differences and enable their meaning-making. This only happens if the "circle is closed "by validating their interpretation of materials, and interdisciplinary literature is a beginning. Checking and discussing media is a way to ensure the student can disseminate what they have learnt.

Connectivism suggests that students should have some control over what is shared and make platforms for students (Downes and Siemens CCK08), and creating blogs or chat rooms can help the discussion and analysis of those who join in. The tutor and student can benefit by using technology and interpreting academic work. Kennedy et al. (2017) suggest that academics often criticise the lack of academic tone and referencing in students' work.

In summary, there is also an issue where only some students perform well at the beginning of the course, leading academic staff to blame the students for their lack of study skills or the course's recruitment process. Barbazon (2002) notes a need for more emphasis on teaching academic writing skills to students. Overall, educational institutions must recognise the need to provide robust academic writing instruction to students and support them in developing the skills needed to succeed in their academic pursuits.

IN THEIR OWN WORDS

3 USING ARTIFICIAL INTELLIGENCE

In this chapter, I have used ChatGPT for the search through literature. Students in 2023 have been presented with a new way to seek a good work structure using a new tool called ChatGPT (Open AI 2023). There has been an unsettled array of reports and comments about ChatGPT and how it might lead to plagiarism. Still, a tutor can advise students about using ChatGPT, which avoids plagiarism and helps them with their thoughts and analysis. Like using Grammarly, Google Scholar or a reference tool like Mendeley, I would teach new students how to use ChatGPT to analyse their essay structure and decide on its usefulness for their work The chapter begins with instructions on how to use ChatGPT as a research tool and the second part shows an example of work that could be a good academic basis for writing about refugees and maternity issues.

Student Use of ChatGPT.

ChatGPT stands for "Chat Generative Pre-Trained Transformer." It is an artificial intelligence language model developed by Open Artificial Intelligence. It is designed to understand natural language and generate responses to questions or prompts in a human-like manner. ChatGPT uses machine learning algorithms to analyse vast amounts of data and learn from it to generate coherent and contextually relevant responses. It has been trained on various of sources, including books, articles, and websites, and can produce various responses to a given prompt. Https://www.linkedin.com/pulse/understanding-chat-gpt-advantages-growth-prospects-mohindroo-

I am so excited about how this new technology can change teaching and learning. A good place to start exploring this step change in AI is Stephen Atlas's book ChatGPT for Higher Education, found at https://digitalcommons.uri.edu/cgi/viewcontent.cgi?article=1547&context=cba_facpubs.

How to Start an Enquiry

- Firstly, the enquiry to ChatGPT must be as robust as a Boolean search on the internet. (See later chapters if you are unclear about Boolean searches). "Analyse" is a better word than "describe" or "list" for academic searches in ChatGPT. Once you have a short list of pros and cons, you could enter some of the terms into Google Scholar to see what you should read about for your essay.

- Secondly, the answers, in this case, the pros and cons of ChatGPT, are listed. Do not take them all. Use what is relevant to your enquiry or research.

- Thirdly, do further research. Enter the sentences from the answers on ChatGPT to different search engines. Make sure you have them all by using the sentences again into a Google Scholar search to find papers that have been peer-reviewed.

- Fourthly, review the references as you do for any other source. References are listed and stripped for details that can be used in the discussion about ChatGPT.

- Lastly, the student gets to work, using their references to construct a write-up of the issue. Students must structure their writing to provide a point, evidence or reference and expand. (PEE). Then the student adds an introduction and conclusion to their work.

- The tutor can put a work section into ChatGPT and ask, "Did you write this?" ChatGPT can say "yes" if the student did not work on it and use it as an entry point, not a whole essay.

Example of the Lists You Could Make From a Search Using ChatGPT.

The subject for this section is "The pros and cons of using ChatGPT".
Using ChatGPT for research has several potential benefits but also some drawbacks. Here are some pros and cons to consider:
This video shows students how to start using this app. Https://www.yaaka.cc/what-is-chatgpt/

Pros of ChatGPT:
- *Accessibility*: ChatGPT can be accessed from anywhere with an internet connection, making it a convenient tool for researchers who may not have access to traditional research facilities or libraries. Now Put this through Google Scholar; you have a paper or two to read, such as Dwivedi et al. (2023).

- *Efficiency*: ChatGPT can process large amounts of text data in a relatively short time, making it an efficient tool for research. To add to this persuasive argument, read the paper suggested by google Scholar. To snowball the research read the references in the paper given by Google Scholar. Haleem al (2023) writes about efficiency and a lot more to add to the analysis of ChatGPT.

- *Cost-effective*: Using ChatGPT for research can be more cost-effective than hiring a team of researchers, especially for smaller projects. Further enquiries may turn up (Alshater, 2022).

- *Objectivity*: ChatGPT can objectively analyse text data, as it is not influenced by human biases or subjectivity. Again, do not leave this at one search look further using this sentence. Finding newer papers is vital such as Jungwirth and Haluza (2023).

- *Versatility*: ChatGPT can be used for various research purposes, from text analysis to natural language processing. Search further for Atlas (2023).

Now do the same for the cons of ChatGPT.

Cons of ChatGPT:
- *Accuracy*: While ChatGPT is highly accurate in many cases, it is not infallible, and its results may be subject to errors and inaccuracies. New search has turned up a newer paper by Atlas, (2023).

- *Reliability*: Because ChatGPT is an AI-based tool, its reliability may be subject to technical issues or data bias. Newer research is found using the sentence provided by Chat GPT;(Thurzo,et al 2023) (Strunga et al., 2023).

- *Limitations*: ChatGPT may have limitations when it comes to analysing certain types of data or languages that it has yet to be trained on. Put this sentence into a search engine and get Kocoń (2023).

- *Lack of human insight*: ChatGPT objective analysis may lack the depth of insight that human researchers can provide. (Farrokhnia, et al 2023).

- *Ethics*: Using ChatGPT for research may raise ethical concerns about privacy and data security. Google Scholar will give you papers to read for your research now that you have clear terms to search. (Tlili 2023).

The student must then be taught to make a storyboard or series of points to discuss using their up-to-date reading from Google Scholar or the universities library search tools. Many leave their references raw by just putting the reference behind their statements. The skill is to embed the author's name into the text showing a mastery of what was written about. Academics /students must be taught to read and skim what is said in their papers and then reference.

If a student's writing gets too wordy and mixed up, they could paste it into Grammarly for checks or ChatGPT for rewording. The student must still read it to ensure it matches their enquiry or essay. I always check for plagiarism, as ChatGPT might get a lot from one website! Turnitin or Grammarly will check for plagiarism.

Using ChatGPT for research can be a useful and cost-effective tool for analysing large amounts of text data. However, knowing its limitations and potential drawbacks is important when using it as part of a research project.

Consider the following section, "Maternity experiences of refugee women". It is an enquiry that ChatGPT wrote. The headings are useful for structuring your work and show how themes could be made from the literature. Currently, ChatGPT is on version 4, so it would not be considered reliable for references. Useful to structure arguments and consider the Point before you provide Evidence and Expand. PEE is encouraged in all academic writing and is considered a good structure.

I put it through 'Grammarly', which had many grammar faults, but I was pleased to see it had not plagiarised any websites.

IN THEIR OWN WORDS

Maternity Experiences of Refugee Women – A Piece Written Using ChatGPT

Title: Refugee Women and Maternity Services in the UK

Abstract: The United Kingdom (UK) has received many refugees in recent years, including women. These women face numerous challenges, including accessing adequate healthcare services, particularly during pregnancy and childbirth. This paper reviews the literature on refugee women's experiences in UK maternity services and identifies their challenges and barriers. The findings reveal that refugee women have limited access to appropriate care due to language barriers, cultural differences, and discrimination. The paper concludes by calling for greater attention to the needs of refugee women in UK maternity services and the development of policies and interventions that address the barriers they face.

Introduction: The UK has a long history of receiving refugees, and in recent years, there has been a significant increase in the number of refugees seeking asylum in the country. Many of these refugees are women who face numerous challenges, including accessing adequate healthcare services, particularly during pregnancy and childbirth. Maternity services are an essential component of healthcare for pregnant women, and the failure to provide good care can result in adverse maternal and foetal outcomes.

Literature Review: The literature on refugee women's experiences in UK maternity services is limited, but it highlights the challenges and barriers they face. Language barriers are a significant obstacle to accessing appropriate care, as many refugee women have limited proficiency in English. Al-Ramahi et al. (2018) found that language barriers often lead to miscommunication and misunderstandings between healthcare providers and refugee women. The study also found that refugee women were less likely to receive appropriate care due to language barriers.

Cultural differences are another significant barrier to accessing appropriate care. For example, refugee women may have different expectations and beliefs about pregnancy and childbirth compared to UK-born women, which healthcare providers may not understand or accommodate. For example, a study by Higginbottom et al. (2019) found that refugee women often had different beliefs about pain and medication use during childbirth, which healthcare providers did not always understand or accommodate.

Discrimination is another significant barrier to accessing appropriate care. Refugee women may face discrimination based on ethnicity, religion, or immigration status. A study by Bradby et al. (2015) found that refugee women experienced discrimination and racism from healthcare providers, often resulting in delays or denials of care.

Conclusion: Refugee women in the UK face numerous challenges in accessing appropriate care during pregnancy and childbirth. The challenges include language barriers, cultural differences, and discrimination. The failure to provide adequate care can result in adverse maternal and foetal outcomes. To address these challenges, there is a need for greater attention to the needs of refugee women in UK maternity services. In addition, policies and interventions should be developed to address refugee women's barriers, including providing interpreter services, culturally sensitive care, and anti-discrimination training for healthcare providers.

4 RESEARCH METHODOLOGY

The previous chapter demonstrates the shortcomings of using a tool like ChatGPT to fulfil the requirement to conduct research with refugee women. I will now explain the steps I underwent to conduct research with this target group.

Setting Up Your Research

Description of the methodology used in a particular piece of research should have the following components:

1. *Introduction*: Provide an overview of the research question, objectives, and hypotheses, as well as the rationale for using a particular methodology.
2. *Research design:* Describe the overall research design, including the research approach, data collection methods, and sampling strategy. Discuss how the design aligns with the research question and objectives.
3. *Data collection*: Detail the methods used, including any instruments or tools used to collect data and any ethical considerations considered.
4. *Data analysis*: Explain the methods, including any statistical or qualitative techniques employed. Discuss how the data analysis aligns with the research question and objectives.
5. *Limitations*: Acknowledge any limits to the methodology, including potential biases, issues with the sample or data collection methods, and any constraints on the study.
6. *Conclusion*: Summarise the methodology used, highlighting its strengths and limitations. Discuss how the methodology contributes to answering the research question and objectives.
7. *Appendices*: Include any supplemental materials such as survey questionnaires, interview protocols, or consent forms used in the study.

Well-written pieces should provide enough detail and clarity so that other researchers can replicate the study. It should also demonstrate that the methodology is appropriate for the research question and objectives and that the findings can be trusted.

The best number for a survey about refugee women will depend on several factors, including the specific research objectives, available resources, and the population size of the target group (refugee women in this case). To ensure the survey results accurately reflect the experiences and perspectives of refugee women, it is important to have a sample size that is large enough to provide a representative sample of the population. This typically involves sampling a proportionate number of participants from different subgroups within the population (e.g., different refugee backgrounds, ages, and socioeconomic statuses).

A larger sample size generally increases the statistical power of the survey, allowing for more precise estimates and more decisive conclusions. However, the required sample size for adequate statistical power will depend on factors such as the expected effect size, confidence level, and the desired margin of error. Conducting surveys can be resource-intensive, requiring time, personnel, and financial resources. Considering the available resources and feasibility of data collection within the given constraints is essential. For most research modules, you are evidencing that you can conduct research, so the actual results are less important than the way you found them, and you do not need to impress with numbers. The more answers you get, the more work you must do on number crunching. The anticipated response rate should be considered when determining the sample size. A larger sample size may be necessary to compensate for potential non-response bias if the response rate is low.

Researchers should also consider the ethical implications of the study, ensuring that the survey is designed in a way that respects the privacy and confidentiality of the participants.

Ultimately, there is no "best" number for a survey about refugee women. The sample size should be determined by carefully assessing the specific research goals, resources, and practical considerations. It may be beneficial to consult a statistician or research methodologist to determine an appropriate sample size that balances representativeness, statistical power, and feasibility.

Research Methods -design

The data collection was between September and December 2022.

Phase one was a group of parents at "Let's Play" as a pilot (N=30)

Phase two was previous and presented "Let's Play" parents (N=12)

Phase three was a follow-up to babies born during COVID-19 in a refuge for asylum-seeking women. (N=11)

Phase four was an invite to the Carriers of Hope baby help project for every baby born in 2022 (N= 27)

The design was qualitative to gain insight into the experiences of the women. A mapping exercise identified a cohort of women who had used Carriers of Hope to support their children.

Research methods were tailored to the individual circumstances of the women involved, and whichever way the women wanted to be approached for their story was utilised. The women disclosed only what they wished and could choose the venue and time of their interview. In this way, it is likely to reduce the researcher's power. This practice of inclusive work with refugees and asylum seekers dictates that the research is not bound by red tape or rigid since this will not serve the participants well. Euro-centric ways of research where one method will fit all are not recommended by researchers with experience working with people of refugee backgrounds.

The researcher included group work and one-to-one conversations at home and considered talking on the phone or via Zoom. Carriers of Hope have an active set of befrienders recruited from the regular clients at the "Let's Play" Parents and Toddlers activity group (Learning English Together Through Play). These played a vital role in the research, especially where translation is needed. White, middle-class, privileged and educated workers need help connecting to disadvantaged women with various issues. Culturally appropriate work must include refugees in positions of power within the research. Research relies on dialogue, which can be very slow and misinterpreted when working with refugees and asylum seekers. Hence, women need to talk to other women as interpreters and advocates.

Questions Included Semi-Structured Interview Questions

1. Thoughts and feelings when you found out you were pregnant
2. Any thoughts about health care throughout the pregnancy
3. The birth and post-natal support for your baby.

Sample Frame

The study was undertaken in Coventry, England, with refugee and asylum-seeking women aged 19-36, who were gathered into focus groups or interviewed separately from October to December 2022. Most of the groups and interviews had been held at the Hillfields Church, where they attended "Let's Play" sessions with their under-fives. Some interviews occurred in homes, and information was added to informal chats during the play sessions.

Recruitment

After a phone call, ten visits were carried out in the third data collection home. In this group, there were five English speakers, half the group. Two Kurdish Sorami speakers used their boyfriends to translate for this study, one Vietnamese woman who managed to speak using her phone as a translator and two Albanian who translated for each other.

Methods

The interviews were in English and were all undertaken by the same researcher, Dr Lin Armstrong, with the help of interpreters from the focus group. In addition, a second record keeper/note taker was recruited from the group, and notes from the researcher and note taker were discussed immediately after the session.

Ethics

Having explained the purpose of the study, the researcher obtained informed consent from all participants, who were made aware that their participation was entirely voluntary and that they were free to withdraw from the study at any time and that any information they provided would be anonymised to ensure confidentiality. Pseudonyms were used to protect the identity of participants.

All women were informed with written and spoken information in their language. Once they agreed to participate, an appointment was arranged at the church. Only one interview was undertaken through a Skype call. The researcher was available to speak with women who wanted to participate in the study. They were provided with the participant information sheet, translated into Arabic. As a result, the participants were reminded that participation was voluntary, and only those who provided written consent participated in the study. Most women held their babies during the interviews, which lasted 25-35 min. All of the interviews were conducted by the first author and the interpreter in Arabic, Tigrigna, in an appropriate and culturally respectful way.

5 CREATING A SURVEY FOR USE WITH REFUGEE WOMEN

The previous chapter demonstrates the shortcomings of using a tool like ChatGPT to fulfil the requirement to conduct research with refugee women. I will now explain the steps I underwent to conduct research with this target group. The question was," What would the women like to do in their group with the charity?"

Theory
Researching with, rather than on, refugee women is crucial for several reasons. Firstly, it recognises the importance of the voices and experiences of those being studied. Refugees are often marginalised, and their perspectives are frequently overlooked or dismissed. By involving them in the research process, we can ensure their insights are heard and considered, leading to more accurate and valuable findings.

Secondly, researching refugee women can help to build trust and foster meaningful relationships between researchers and participants. Refugees may be understandably wary of outsiders and uncomfortable sharing their experiences or perspectives. Researchers can create a more supportive and inclusive environment by working collaboratively with them, leading to more honest and open discussions.

Thirdly, researching with refugee women can help address power imbalances in traditional research relationships. Historically, research has been conducted by outsiders who hold all the power, while participants are often seen as passive recipients of information. We can challenge this dynamic by involving refugees in research and creating an equal partnership.

Finally, researching refugee women can help to ensure that research findings are relevant and applicable to their needs. Refugee women face unique challenges and experiences often overlooked in traditional research. By involving them in the research process, we can better understand their experiences and develop more effective interventions and policies tailored to their needs.

When constructing the questions for a survey for refugee women, several factors should be considered to ensure that your survey effectively gathers the information you need while being culturally sensitive and respectful of their experiences.

I suggest the following key aspects for consideration:
1. *Purpose and goals*: Clearly define the purpose of your survey and what information you hope to gather from refugee women. This will help you determine the questions you must ask and the data type you want to collect.
2. *Cultural sensitivity:* Consider the cultural and social backgrounds of the refugee women you target with your survey. Make sure that your questions are culturally sensitive, and avoid any language that may be offensive or insensitive.
3. *Language barriers*: If you are conducting a survey in a language other than your own, ensure you have someone who can translate the questions accurately to ensure the refugee women understand them.

4. *Demographic data*: Collect demographic data, such as age, ethnicity, and education level, to help you better understand the backgrounds of the refugee women you are surveying.
5. *Types of questions*: Use a mix of open-ended and closed-ended questions to get a range of responses. Closed-ended questions can provide quantitative data, while open-ended questions allow for more in-depth and qualitative responses.
6. *Sensitivity of the questions*: Be mindful of the sensitivity of your questions, especially regarding topics such as trauma, abuse, and sexual violence. Consider offering respondents an option to skip questions they may find uncomfortable or triggering.
7. *Pilot testing:* Before conducting the survey, conduct a pilot test with a small group of refugee women to ensure the questions are clear, understandable, and culturally appropriate.

Considering these factors, you can create a survey that effectively collects the information you need from refugee women.

Practice

My purpose was to design a survey to find out what the women wanted to learn about and discuss in a new group which would focus on helping them to address the issues which were of the greatest importance to them.

My starting point was to bring together a smaller group of 5 women who have children and to have some open sharing of ideas, opinions, what they had found helpful over their time with Carriers of Hope, what they wanted more of and what they thought that other women in a similar position would need to know about.

Their answers were very insightful and informative and would lead to creating a questionnaire which I could use with a much wider cohort of women, as a Google survey sent to their phones.

This is what the initial group said:

1) We probably need an induction for the moms as you did in the beginning when we come to Coventry because new mums are coming or having babies this year, and they do not know about babies or where to take them.
2) We need English classes like you did before.
3) It was always the best thing for us to get out of the rooms when we were new mums, and it would cheer us up. (Brenda, Mum of 1 year old in hostel)
4) Mostly the need is language and how to communicate.
5) Befriending - no one wants to go out because of language.
6) Sometimes you are put in a house where others know the schools and hospitals and give advice. They need to be taken along. They don't know how to read or write. They do not know what the Home Office is saying or what they are getting. They become stagnant and can't move their family forward. We need a project that can expand life. The Home Office puts people in Bed and Breakfast for eight weeks or more, and during this time, they do appointments and details of documents, then they can put you anywhere far away from anyone you know. They move lots to Birmingham and then move them again, and again. The church is essential to get a family. They can give you food and money to travel. People arrive without family, just their child, and they must fit into the community but do not know how to. They need a communication project. (Gloria, mum of a 7-year-old living in shared housing)
7) We need support networks; you need to know someone to get food and clothes
8) Then being a volunteer is good, ready for work if they pay your bus fare.
9) Education. in Africa, you may have little education, especially as a girl, so we need to know how to continue our education, seek help and get ideas for work.
10) Knowledge, we need the courses to get into education to get there. We need to learn at home how to support our claims.
11) Children need help in the years before starting school (Anita lives in a house with two children and also has children back in Africa)
12) Children's project

13) Education that leads to what to do after coming here. The English language is needed because they are shy to come out because they can't speak—my friend worries about coming to the playgroup. After all, she can't speak English. (Rada family with two children now has the right to remain and work.)

Once this pilot phase was completed, a series of questions were created from the above, that were translated into Kurdish and Arabic, as well as English, to aim to find out what additional help should be available for women refugees.

The survey

Hello, we at Carriers of Hope want to know what you need. Please fill in this form by filling in some information, and by ticking those which are most important, and you would attend online or in the Hillfields church.

Which languages do you speak? ………………………………………
How old are your children? ………………………………………

Please tick the important things from this list
Children's information to be posted onto WhatsApp or covered in a group
Healthy cooking
Safe sleeping
Weaning
Food hygiene
How to teach your child through play
Understanding your child's behaviour
Information about health issues
Women's information to be posted onto WhatsApp or delivered at the sessions
Introduction to services in Coventry
Meeting women from your own country
English classes with your baby
Information about English classes in Coventry
Nursery and school information
Help to go to services.
Help to read and reply to letters and forms
Information about churches
How to continue your adult education in Coventry

Anything else that you need? ……………………………………………………………………………
……
……
……

Helplines
If you need help with clothing, please use this Coventry Clothing helpline
If you have problems getting food
If you need household goods

6 WRITING UP THE RESULTS OF THE MATERNITY RESEARCH

Women from asylum-seeking and refugee backgrounds are often described as "hard to reach", but by using Carriers of Hope, a Non-governmental organisation, a sample of 53 women was included in this report. The methodology used was to set up focus groups and interviews with women so the delivery of maternity services could be examined.

I conducted this community research to assess and improve care for women with babies and children.

When writing up qualitative data from raw results, you typically follow these steps:
1. Organise the data: The raw data is organised into categories, themes, or codes. This will help you identify patterns and trends in the data.
2. Identify key quotes: Go through the data and identify critical quotes that illustrate your identified categories or themes.
3. Analyse the data: Analyse the quotes and data to identify emerging common themes or patterns. Look for similarities, differences, or trends that you can use to develop your analysis.
4. Develop your analysis: Develop your analysis by drawing connections between the data and your research question or objectives. Use the quotes and data to support your claims and arguments.
5. Provide context for your analysis by discussing the cultural, historical, or social factors that may have influenced the data.
6. Use examples from the data to support your claims and arguments. Be sure to include quotes and other data to illustrate your points.
7. Discuss limitations: Discuss any limitations or weaknesses of your analysis, such as sample size or potential biases in the data.
8. Conclude: Draw conclusions based on your analysis of the data. Discuss the implications of your findings for theory, practice, or future research.

When writing up qualitative data, it is essential to be systematic and exact in your analysis. Use the raw data (what the women say) to support your claims and arguments, and be transparent about your methods and limitations. I always check my codes and themes to ensure I am interpreting the data correctly. Once you know what the women say, two themes can be put together under one heading, such as words about poverty issues can be added together.

What did Women Say? The Maternity Experiences of Women at Carriers of Hope

The funding from Health Watch that enabled this research is timely and much needed. In 2021, almost half of all live births in Coventry were to mothers born outside of the UK, this made up 45.2% of all live births in the city. This trend continues.

Women from asylum-seeking and refugee backgrounds are often described as "hard to reach", but by reaching women at Carriers of Hope, a sample of 53 women was included in this report. The methodology used was to set up focus groups and interviews with women so the delivery of maternity services could be examined.

Phase one was a group of parents at "Let's Play" as a pilot (N=30)
Phase two was previous and present "Let's Play" parents (N=12)
Phase three was a follow-up to babies born during COVID-19 in a refuge for asylum-seeking women. (N=11)

Messages from Research. What do women say about maternity care?

Before the Birth

<u>Difficulty in accessing support services</u>: One issue is finding the actual services "*I was moved here from London, my husband could sleep at his work, but there was no room for me being pregnant.*"

Immigration status affects how women receive help. Asylum legislation rules will affect if a woman can access maternity services. For example, one woman in this group had been charged for her first birth at £6,000. Although pregnant again, she would not be presenting to her GP because she could not afford the birth.

The women discussed how Immigration status affects women; they all knew about hidden pregnancies and have friends who become late bookers or non-bookers, giving birth at home and avoiding midwives and health visitors.

<u>Confusion over primary, secondary, and tertiary health care roles</u>: The group is most vulnerable to missing communication about their health services. The lead-up to the birth was one of confusion for Arabic speakers. They mixed up midwives with health visitors in their relaying of their stories. In one of the focus groups, 6 women reported they had seen the midwife first: 4 reported they saw the doctor first, and 2 said they presented themselves at the hospital as soon as they found out they were pregnant. No one in Focus groups 1 or 2 knew their health visitors' names, even the English speakers. *'Every month, there is a new midwife; they call in other staff constantly'* "*Once I learned a name because she said 'Hi, I am Sarah,' but she did not come again.*" "They are short-staffed, so whoever can come will come."

<u>A lack of compassion:</u> One Arabic speaker said she was rushed to the hospital on the bus; her husband could not come because they had other children that he needed to look after. Her waters broke and she told the staff she was in labour and needed pain control. They said, "*This shift ends in ten minutes, so you just have to wait for the next shift.*" This lady gave birth sooner than the staff expected and inconvenienced the team. "*It was a strong baby and pushed out before she finished her shift*"

One woman who had a previous baby born dead said the receptionist at the hospital shouted at her because she should speak English. It was difficult to say what had happened, and she had no English for it. This topic brought laughter from the rest of the group, who said they had the same!

The women never complained and did not know they could. They laughed at the way *"The receptionists think they are doctors "*. There seemed to be a lack of confidentiality between the receptionist and two of the women. *"Yeah, they shout you out in front of the whole waiting list "*. Women also reported that the receptionists in the hospital *"are not happy, are not smiling"*. There was a discussion about whether they were under pressure because they are sometimes rude.

In FG2 and 3, the women agreed that "*you can press the bell with pain, and it always takes 15 minutes to respond*". They agreed that the staff need more help because "*they are so tired*". One woman at Birmingham Hospital said she loved the staff and helped them out. She could speak English, so she was able "*to help the mummies*".

<u>Communication difficulties:</u> The frustrations at passing information onto medical teams, the women say, are sometimes because their husband or child is interpreting for them, and they do not know the English for pregnancy terms.

Translations and interpretations are very hit-and-miss throughout the services. The women feel they need an interpreter from the start as women usually speak less English. *'I take my husband to the hospital, but he can't come every time'*. Translators are in the hospital sometimes, but often the women do not get the appointment times right as the receive hospital appointment letters in English. One woman with diabetes had no money for her hospital appointment, but she knew it was important. A lack of clarity in the English forms limited her ability to reclaim the bus fare. She asked Carriers of Hope to give her a lift there but found that her baby's father had mistranslated the appointment time. The translator was booked for two hours later and was not available. The hospital staff discussed that she had missed two appointments and should not have any more. *"You are at risk! You should come to your appointments"*, (the receptionist loudly told her).

The women were often asked by staff why they could not learn some English to help their children and their pregnancy, not realising the cultural situation. that in some countries, education is for boys. Boys learn English, and girls move out to live in another family. (Sudan) *"Women do not go to school in my country"*.

They all had a "Red book" given to them on the ward. *"They are in English, but the pictures help "*. No-one used their book but had it somewhere in case they go to weigh their baby. One woman, an English speaker in FG2, said that since Covid, there was a green book online, but it was in English.

Many participants felt underprepared for the birth, but one woman felt differently. She had watched You tube in her language and gained much knowledge about caring for herself and her baby.

<u>Specific difficulties for the Muslim women:</u> Many births caused embarrassment for the women when they needed a doctor because the Muslim women don't accept being attended by a man, and they had to ask their husbands if a male doctor could attend to them. This is a cause of anxiety.

<u>The Effect of Poverty:</u> The support available needs to be clarified regarding the costs of having a baby. The women's answers varied as each woman reported what they claimed. *"£51 for two kids every month"*; *"I had no money"*. Other women said she could have got £500 at the birth. She thought she had applied but never got it. The women argued amongst themselves that there were benefits to be claimed. *"£14 a week every Monday for five children"*; *"£21 a week for one child"* An English speaker explained it depends on your circumstances and status as an asylum seeker. *"Like how long your case has been going on "*. *"I get £17 for two children "."* *If your husband has an EU passport like my husband has, you can get an English one, you can get the £500"*, and more misconceptions were voiced *"If you come from Paris to here, you are not working. You can get the money for the first baby"* This was refuted by the Africans who said," *You can get up to two children now - not for a third or fourth"*.

There was similar confusion over a healthy start voucher.

"It is for milk and fruit for your baby ". One lady had lost her PIN, so she never claimed it. Another cannot remember being given a card, and another said she did not get one in the hospital.

Poor housing worried them about hyperthermia, so they used many layers of blankets until Carriers of Hope supplied sleep suits and guidance about safer sleeping. All of the women reported that they live in overcrowded poor conditions. One woman lives in a hotel with her husband and five children in two rooms.

The women had received their baby things and hospital bags from Carriers of Hope, and without these, they would be on the ward without clothes, wash items or a car seat to take the baby home. *"You cannot leave unless you have a car seat." "Yes, they are £70 in Argos!"*. One participant had a husband that worked, so he paid for their equipment. *"But he doesn't have a job now, so we need a bed for my son "*. This started a list of needs *"I need vests; I need a pram; I need clothes for my baby"*. All were referred to Carriers of Hope's helpline.

<u>The value of a group of friends:</u> The importance of knowing other women repeatedly arose because they could share information, for example, tell women about helplines and support them. They also share resources *"Friends give me a dressing gown, nice"*. Relying on friends to tell them about travel to the hospital is the norm.

The woman living in a hotel had nowhere to cook or wash her clothes, so the women helped her by cooking extra when they could. The majority had a husband who could not attend the birth whilst looking after other children at home. One woman took a friend to the birth of her first child. The women from Eritrean all relied on one woman with poor English to translate for them in the group but conveyed that they had husbands that could translate in the hospital - if they could get there.

<u>The lack of power:</u> FG1 discussed fears about their health care and the lack of power to voice their concerns. They all said when you are pregnant, your doctor tells you, *"It is normal in pregnancy"*, and *"You cannot tell your doctor you are sick even when he should check or investigate. He sends you home"*. The fears were brushed off. *"You might have a malfunction of a child deformed in pregnancy, and you get sent home anyway."*

There was an opinion from African women that the doctor *"thinks I can manage pain - I cannot."* Two women said their discomfort of being wet, itching, or discharging was not normal pregnancy, but they were sent away from the doctors without investigation. One reported, *"The passage had bacteria that could have made my child deaf from infection"*.

Their Birth Experience in Hospital

<u>Interactions with the staff:</u> In general, the women were pleased with the hospital ward staff. *"They were always around you"*. All women, except one, have given birth in UHCW, Coventry. *"The hospital is better than in my country!"*

D. was grateful for her hospital stay this time. Her first baby was born during Covid, and she was moved into a refuge from Newcastle without money or food, so she could not breastfeed him. Her baby was three weeks early, and she attended the hospital with a booked interpreter. Her babies are tiny at 2 kilos, but she could only stay in the hospital for two days. *"The treatment was to make the baby born early at 11 pm night-time."* She told me. Her boyfriend was allowed to see her in the hospital and brought his first child in to see her. She gave birth alone since they had no childcare, but she felt confident and was keen to say, *"The staff were a good help when I rang the bell"* Other women had said the bell rang and rang, and no one came.

One woman repeatedly asked for an epidural to relieve pain, but she never got one.

"I had a bed beside the office, so I heard them discussing me, saying I was strong. I was not feeling strong; I had pain; my breastfeeding was going well, so they sent me home. I had no experience caring for a baby, so I was frightened to return to the hotel." The nurse said, *'Let's wait; night staff can decide. I do not want the blame for putting her out of bed'*. The other nurse said, *"I don't want to take the rap either. Let's wait, and the night staff can decide!"* This lady was sent home at 10 pm; she was in a hotel room alone with her new baby until the staff got her food.

The high-stress environment of the maternity unit and the challenges faced led to bullying in the hospital wards. *"I was on Wards 24 and 25 for five days. The night staff were made up of older women who were rude and bullied some women there. One lady wanted help with breastfeeding, and they went back to their desk and said, "It's not rocket science; she should have got it by now"*. *"They did not like to attend to anyone but talked very loudly to keep us awake. Some ladies had a very rough time."* (R).

"I wouldn't dare to tell them I needed their help!" (B).

"I was at home and had no money to get the bus to the hospital. My baby came out, so a neighbour called the ambulance." This woman reports she was in the hospital for just 3 hours before they sent her home again. Within hours of being at home with her new baby, she could not walk, so called the ambulance again and was kept in for a week with complications.

The women joined in with the discussion about quick eviction from hospital beds. *"White ladies stay the night!"* *"They think because you are black, you are strong!"* (R and M)

Some avoided the hospital and knew of others who never went.

<u>Communication difficulties:</u> Some thought communication in the hospital was poor like this comment from a woman who had a baby die just before birth; *'I had first baby problems, but they did not know although my husband told them."* The communication barriers were again a big issue. *"Indians are lucky, most of the staff speak Indian languages, and none speak French or Arabic!"*

The Sudanese women explained that Arabic translation is difficult since there are differences in spoken Arabic depending on where they come from

'Interpreters from Syria and Iraq can't understand us, and we can't understand them. So I prefer an interpreter from Sudan [who speaks Sudanese Arabic].'

The women who did not have access to mobile phones of their own reported they could not update their family. Apparently, *"the hospital has a complicated phone system, and they could not ask how I was or when I would come out"* (B). Often, the husbands and boyfriends did not know how their pregnant or birthing wife was doing.

C-sections: *"I gave birth at 3 am, had a C-section and was sent home by 10 pm. SERCO booked a taxi, or I would have to walk home with my new baby"* (R).

After the Birth

Follow-up healthcare: When asked if the health visitor came to their homes to teach them about their new baby, there was a mixture of answers. One said their health visitor came four times, but the majority said three visits, or more if they had a C-section.

The advice from Health visitors was helpful, but some advice went against what they believed about child care. The way that their child-rearing practices differed from the health visitor had the potential to cause tension between health visitors and the women. The notion of routines for the baby was the most significant cause of concern. Their preference was to feed on demand. Carrying the babies was another area of disagreement, for example, the African mothers swung their babies onto their backs to "back them" by wrapping a cloth around the baby and tying them onto their back. *"They said they watched how I lifted my son and said it was aggressive; the Africans are like this; it's how they go."*

Another woman said, *"The health visitor came to talk to me about how I handle my child. My mother handled me that way when I was growing up. Is there anything wrong with me? Why do they think their way is the only way? I am not going to break my daughter's arm, I love her, but no, the workers, they don't see it that way; they said I was rough"*. (S)

One woman said the co-sleeping of her baby was not permitted by the health visitor, but she did it anyway since the house was cold and she worried about her child dying. She lied to the health services to cover her "bad parenting".

The discussions then centred around the fact that follow-up care and health services could help you as a new parent. An English-speaking African woman said, *"You will have a centre for child health near where you live."* This surprised the women in the group. The woman living in a hotel with five children enquired where hers was as she had never gone with her baby. Three participants reflected they could not walk after the baby, so they never went to weigh the baby.

The Harmony Hub and Hope Centre were given as places to have your baby weighed, but it was decided you need to speak English to book, so of no use to this cohort.

Muslim boy babies should be circumcised early, but the parents could not afford the £500 to get this procedure, which saddened them. Others suggested men in Birmingham that would do this for half the price.

Breastfeeding: It was apparent that most of the women interviewed needed help to understand breastfeeding messages fully. Only one woman in FG1 and two in the home interviews, all with good English, appreciated the importance of breastfeeding a new baby. Observation of the breastfeeding technique may help mothers in this stage. No-one observed these women and helped them to get the latch and position correct.

Breastfeeding dropped off rapidly for the majority of women. The reasons were; *"the baby was probably allergic to me because she vomited milk"*. *"The baby liked the bottle best - she sucked it better"*. *"My child would not accept breast milk"*.

It became clear that babies with tongue ties cannot suck, but the mothers could not afford the £300 to get them cut, and they are not entitled to NHS intervention, so babies remain tongue-tied.

In the home interviews with women who had seen the same health visitor for a year after the birth there was evidence of longer breastfeeding practices from 6 months to two years after the birth.

When moving to bottle feeding most of those interviewed used Aptamil. *"SMA is white baby's milk but gives black babies constipation, so black children are better off on Aptamil."*

Post-natal Depression: Depression, after birth was an issue for many of the women, and this seems to be underdiagnosed since many women did not tell their doctors. A specific problem of cultural differences needs to be taken into account as they have concerns about stigma. (B)

4 of the women admitted that they avoid initiating medical contact, under-report, or minimise symptoms. *"I did tell the doctor in the end because I was afraid I would do something to myself, but I dumped the tablets"* (R).

"I was told of a group for mental health that you ring up, but they were full, so I never rang again"

"There was a woman in our refuge. She took more drugs and slept through all her babies crying." This baby was scalded on the foot by a bottle warmer on the floor as his mother slept.

The black women responded to the question about post-natal depression with a discussion about shame and the disgrace of it. The stigma in Africa made them uncomfortable about having a mental illness, which could be seen as a personal failure or disgrace showing failure and weakness. *"Lazy women should get themselves together and put their baby first"* (A)

Babies' health: The need to work can get in the way of health care appointments such as getting the children inoculated. Some women work such long hours and shifts that they neglect to take their children to check-ups. There was also an issue with the transience of refugee and asylum-seeking women when finding their local services. One had been rehoused twice and hadn't kept a relationship going with their health visitor. R's child is not speaking at 2, nearly 3, and she thinks she should find a place to take him. Another needed support for their two-year-old, who was not growing well, but they did not know where to take her.

Conclusions

The discussions and conclusions drawn from the women's research narratives highlight several important issues and potential interventions to improve access to maternity care for refugee and asylum-seeking women. Here are the key points:

1. *Outdated and fragmented information*: The women's mobility and frequent changes in accommodation make it challenging to maintain accurate and up-to-date professional lists. This hampers their access to care as different charities and services hold separate lists, creating confusion and duplication. Interventions are needed to ensure that information is centralised, regularly updated, and effectively communicated across various organisations.

2. *Negative attitudes and cultural insensitivity*: non-English speaking women face barriers due to negative mindsets and a lack of cultural sensitivity from healthcare providers. Understanding and addressing cultural differences and providing culturally competent care can significantly improve access to and quality maternity services.

3. *Lack of information*: All groups of women, particularly those with linguistic and cultural differences, need more information on accessing maternity services at each journey stage. This lack of knowledge during pregnancy adversely affects their health outcomes. Efforts should be made to provide accurate and accessible information in various languages, especially for women with diverse cultural and linguistic backgrounds.

4. *Health literacy and involvement of men*: Health literacy plays a vital role in maternal health outcomes. Women with lower health literacy are less likely to seek preventive care or attend hospitals for planned appointments. Involving men, who often manage care and communication, in improving health literacy can be an effective intervention. Charities and religious institutions can be utilised to disseminate information and pilot interventions.

5. *Community support and regular meetings*: Building community support sensitive to the lack of maternal health knowledge can be beneficial. Regular, local meetings where women can discuss their issues, receive appropriate referrals, and access basic baby essentials and financial advice can help them build knowledge about the healthcare system and improve their overall well-being.

6. *Understanding women's experiences*: Healthcare workers must know the difficulties women face navigating healthcare systems. Listening to women's perspectives, understanding their previous negative experiences, and addressing their concerns can enhance the quality of care and contribute to better health outcomes.

7. *Barriers related to stress and competing priorities*: Stress, competing priorities, family conflicts, poverty, and reporting to the Home Office are factors that hinder women from making and keeping appointments. Financial challenges, reliance on husbands for transportation, and difficulties arranging childcare lead to missed appointments. Interventions should address these barriers, such as providing financial assistance for transportation or offering flexible appointment scheduling.

8. *Confusion about service costs and eligibility*: Women need clarification about the cost of services and eligibility criteria.

In conclusion, improving access to maternity care for refugee and asylum-seeking women requires addressing multiple factors, including information dissemination, cultural sensitivity, health literacy, community support, and addressing stress-related barriers and competing priorities. However, by implementing targeted interventions and involving various stakeholders, such as healthcare workers, charities, and religious institutions, positive changes can be made to enhance maternal health outcomes for these women and their babies.

Recommendations

1. *Community advocates:* To ensure that the needs of women in the research are effectively addressed, it is crucial to establish advocates or mentors trained to support the community in their languages.
2. *Creating befriending circles*: can be an effective way to disseminate information and provide support. Support groups such as COH, supported with childcare, can also be organised to help women learn English, specifically for pregnancy-related matters. Sharing videos in Arabic and African languages focusing on pregnancy and childcare can also benefit. It is crucial to involve men in these groups to promote inclusivity and comprehensive support.
3. *Relevant communication methods:* In terms of healthcare settings, we recommend that hospitals continue providing information through various communication modes. However, relying solely on electronic methods may marginalise certain groups of women who may need more accessible access to technology or may prefer alternative means of receiving information.
4. *Cultural differences awareness:* Workers must reflect upon intercultural differences between black families and white workers before promoting Eurocentric practices as the best approach. Child-rearing methods of asylum seekers and refugees often differ from the views held by professionals. Attachment theory, commonly taught to professionals, may only sometimes be applicable. Some women believe in communal parenting rather than individual care bonds between mother and baby, especially within certain African families. For instance, leaving children alone or caring for other children may be necessary for some women, but it is not acceptable in Western-oriented parenting styles. It is worth noting that certain rearing practices, such as teaching girls to cook and clean for the family from a young age, are considered valuable within certain cultures and can contribute to their caregiving role for babies.
5. *Counselling:* To provide effective and culturally sensitive counselling, it is essential to have available or mandatory training for counsellors that promotes cultural awareness. Encounters with healthcare staff should be approached as counselling sessions within the framework of continuous care, ensuring the provision of contraceptive advice. It is observed in the study focus groups that women often gather information about contraception from friends and their husbands. However, due to a lack of trust in busy ward environments, women may feel they need to be more empowered to make informed contraceptive choices and exercise contraceptive autonomy.

In summary, it is crucial to prioritise the voices and needs of women in the research by providing appropriate support in their languages, fostering intercultural understanding, involving men in support groups, considering diverse parenting practices, and offering culturally aware counselling. By taking these steps, healthcare professionals can better cater to the unique requirements of these women and promote their overall well-being.

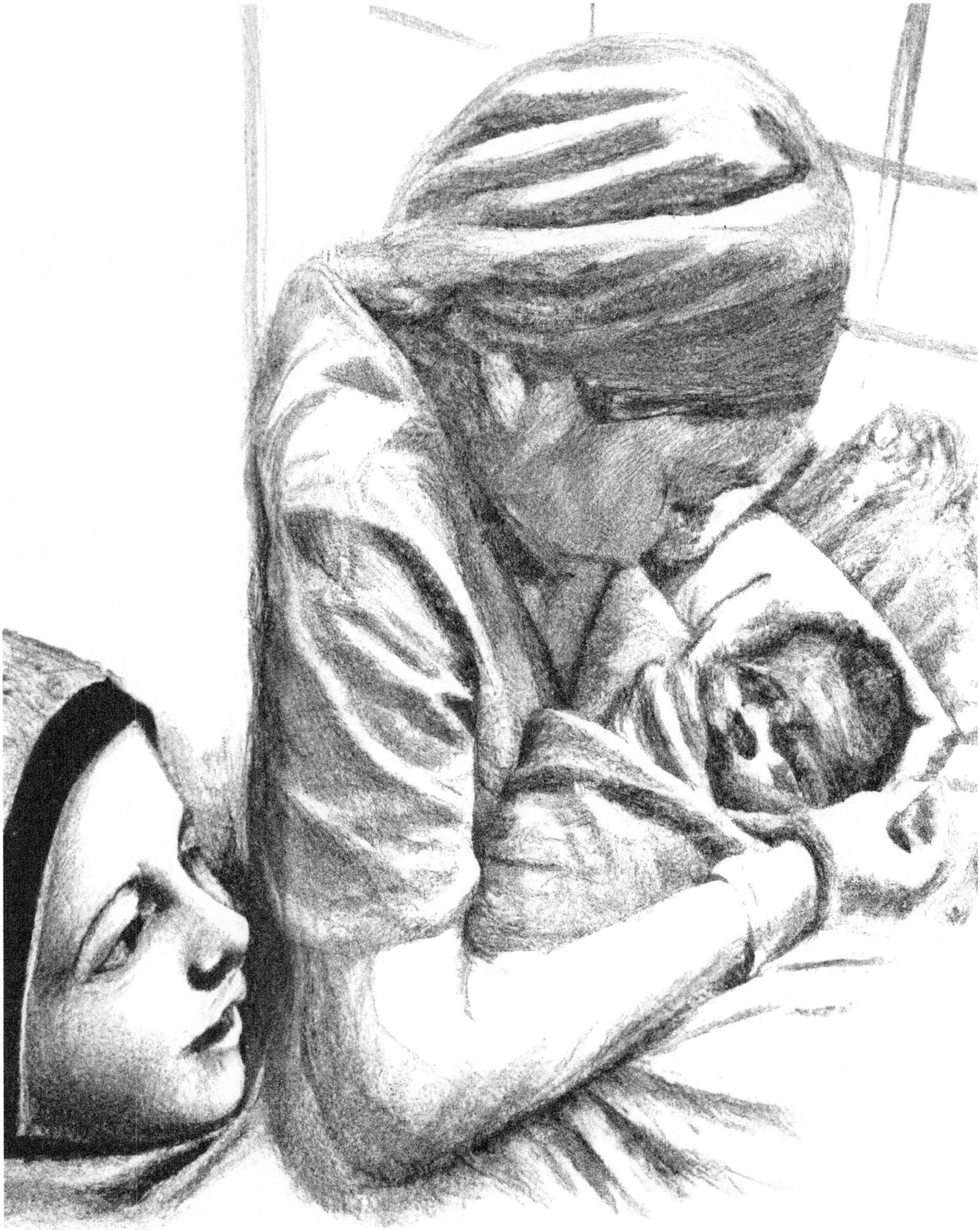

7 PRESENTING ONE'S FINDINGS BY WAY OF A RESEARCH PAPER – "WHAT REFUGEE WOMEN SAY ABOUT THE IMPORTANCE OF SINGING"

This chapter presents a research paper about a singing project with refugee and asylum-seeking children aged 0 to 2 years and their mothers.

Strict ethical guidelines following BERA guidelines were used when researching this vulnerable group.

The singing project came about when Ex Cathedra offered to come to Carriers of Hope's "Let's Play "group to sing with the Mums and work towards a performance at Coventry Cathedral in February. Carriers of Hope have run this group for five years and provide women and young children an opportunity to share songs, learn English and socialise with other families.

While singing with families and young children has always been an essential part of the group, this project brought in a specialist Vocal Tutor from ExCathedra and was funded by Carriers of Hope and ExCathedra. The project is targeted one of the most marginalised groups within communities in Coventry- asylum seekers and refugees. Over three months, the adults and children in Let's Play sang and played with Pippa, a Vocal Tutor from the Ex- Cathedra choir. In addition, Pippa incorporated some creative work into the sessions intending to perform their composition in public at the end of the project. The research revealed that the participants gained a distinct sense of community and belonging through weekly music-making and creativity sessions with their children.

When Let Ex Cathedra and composer Liz Dilnot-Johnson approached's Playleader Alysia to support a song project to be presented at Coventry Cathedral, we recognised an opportunity for research to be undertaken about the collaboration between refugees and creative professionals. These ambitions mirror Carriers of Hope's commitment to the vision that families are welcomed and inspired to rebuild their lives for a better future.

This singing project was distinctive from the usual preschool singing time in several ways;

- The vocal tutor and composer brought children's musical instruments and their instruments, including a harp, a Ukulele, African percussion instruments and other child-friendly percussions.
- Professional musicians led the parents into songs about their food, their hopes for their children, their names, and their favourite things. The songs were about the families in the room from many different cultures.
- The sessions built up leadership capacity allowing the women to lead the songs independently and add their tunes and words together. The professional composer influenced the project but did not lead the song-making.
- The vocal tutor created short videos shared between sessions to help families learn the songs, encourage them to sing with their children at home and build their English vocabulary.
- A direct legacy of the project was to perform in Coventry Cathedral with women and their children on stage and in the video.

Writing a Research Paper

Student researchers must theme the findings when reporting on research to help the reader understand them. For example, this paper's themes were Access and inclusion, Quality of life, Integration, Leadership, Ways of working, Partnerships, and Learning. You might read the data and what you found in your work and list it under different headings. Checking your headings with a supervisor to ensure you report for each section can be helpful.

Writing usually has a broad introduction to ensure the reader knows the research context. The literature is narrowed down in this type of paper. The main findings are what is of interest to other practitioners, and these are themed with clarity. Usually, the recommendations come before any appendices. Since the word count does not include appendices, many students put their details in there and refer to them with analytical points in the main body of the paper.

Sharing research findings with the people who ran the singing group can be seen as an act of courtesy and respect for the work they have done. By sharing the findings with them, you acknowledge their contribution to the project and demonstrate that their efforts have been recognised and valued.

In addition, sharing the research findings with the group leaders can be beneficial in several ways. First, it can help ensure the results are accurately and fairly represented, as the group leaders will likely understand the context and the participants' experiences deeply. They can provide valuable insights and interpretations of the findings that would only be possible with their input.

Second, sharing the findings with the group leaders can help to promote transparency and trust in the research process. By involving them in disseminating the results, you demonstrate a commitment to open communication and a willingness to engage with the people directly involved in the project.

Finally, sharing the findings with the group leaders can ensure that the research has a meaningful impact on the community. For example, the group leaders can use the findings to inform future programming or advocate for singing groups' value to promote social connection and well-being.

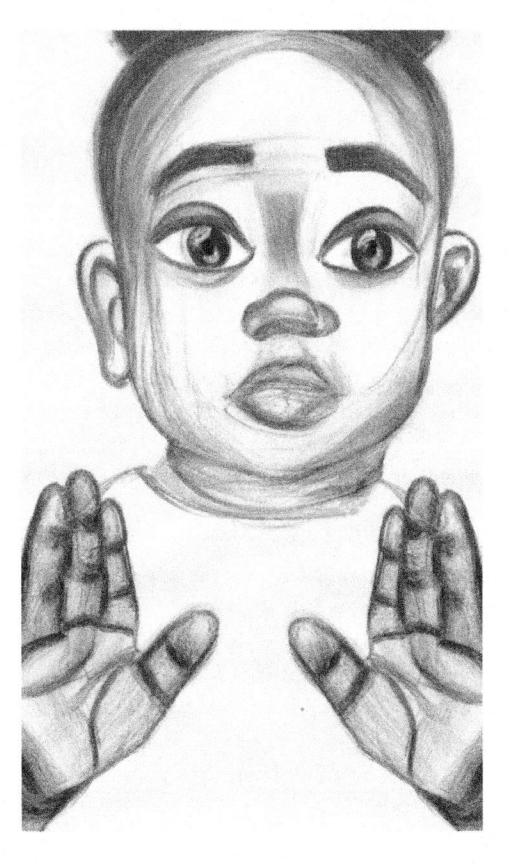

She Shouts Hooray at Bedtime to Get me to Sing the Song
Literature Review

Web of science was searched for the terms Refugee OR asylum-seeking children AND singing. There were no papers suggesting this is a very under-researched area. The next search used the terms Child AND singing AND well-being .16 papers were returned, but not all met the inclusion criteria because they had to be children under five years old. The papers on preschool children and their parents in a group singing activity were lacking, but one from Iceland; Gudmundsdottir (2010), was found. Their parent-infant music classes benefitted young mothers because they increased singing confidence and raised the parents' interest in infants' musical development. This alertness to their child's musical behaviour increased the mother's well-being and mental health. Dinghle (2021) concluded that music activities affect a participant's health and well-being, arousal mood, social connection and physical activity. They all led to relaxation and feeling good about their identity.

Hinshaw, et al (2015.) researched London primary school children and assert their singing group gave positive psychological outcomes to children 7-11.

Wulff, et al (2021) found that music and singing can improve maternal well-being. Their research with 175 pregnant or newly birthed women said the sessions improved infant-child bonding with parents. After each music session stress and mood were measured for each woman and it was improved by singing.

Frimberger, (2016). Showed how a shared singing project leading to a presentation on stage led ESOL learners to feel good about themselves. This was a study with asylum-seeking and refugee backgrounds in Glasgow Scotland. The sessions improved the participant's language competence and showed the English singing teachers a range of songs from the participant's different countries.

The Research Headings

The sample group were 16 to 18 parents, and the primary age of the babies was 0 to 2 years. (n=19). One father was present throughout. The women came from Sudan, Eritrea, Africa, Romania and Iraq. (Kurdish mothers were in the minority, with only two present at times.)

A Mixed-Methods Approach Was Used

A combination of approaches was employed to capture the project's effect in "Let's Play". The refugee women's participatory role in the research highlights good practice in bottom-up information and challenges the power imbalances within research.

The data collection methods included field notes and professional conversations after the music sessions. Interviews were conducted with the vocal tutor, Pippa and composer, Liz.

A focus group was conducted with the parents run by a parent and the researcher. (See Appendix for the Questions used in the Focus Group).

The one-to-one conversations were had with the parents throughout the sessions.

Observations of the children were made through the sessions and later, when parents posted videos of their children to a WhatsApp group, which gave audio and visual evidence of children's enjoyment.

A song was developed with the parents, with assistance from Pippa, so it is their very own song. "Creating our song makes the mums very happy."

Main Findings

The research was embedded in the singing sessions, the WhatsApp group, and parents' discussions. The main findings can be summarised as follows:

Access and inclusion: The music project encouraged new families to join Let's Play. Kurdish participation increased, and isolated families arrived at the Wednesday morning sessions. The songs led to everyone knowing the children's and parents' names. Some of the welcome songs helped the group learn how to sing 'Hello' in different languages. Providing this access to a snack, big play toys and group singing and musical opportunities within the church hall added a distinct sense of community inclusion and belonging. Staff were aware and careful not to stereotype musical preferences or anything like the food used or the names: food was from the mother's own country like "fou fou '"puna yam" and "okara" from Africa and a Sudan mother "Corchorus, Portulaca, cowpea leaves and Eruca."

Furthermore, singing in Coventry Cathedral and inputting to a "Songbook" (a large-format scrapbook of songs) resulted in immense pride and inclusion, according to the focus group participants. Therefore, there is an urgent need for musicians and resources to support, sustain and build on such projects, singing songs and including cultural input from parents. When asked about their performance, some felt there was room for improvement, "The songs stick in their heads but need more polishing". Others complimented the group but observed, "We need proper musicians to back up the mummies, the mummies love to perform, but they need to learn to perform!"

Quality of life. The data from the parents and staff revealed that the singing sessions improved the quality of life and the participants' mental health.

"We all took away great joy from the session". The project provided creative expression and created agency through co-creating and performing. The parents reported that the sessions relieved stress and tension by laughing at their friends dancing and singing. It also promoted pride in their children. "The children made the programme so lovely for the audience."

The loneliness of having a child at home in a tiny room was also mentioned, as was the release, minimising boredom. This was evident when the parents started to post videos of their children singing and playing instruments in the group to show the children at home. The creation of their song, "Made me so happy." Many comments showed the transference of feelings from the mother to the child. "The joy out of me was flown into my baby!"

Some of the parents felt the music helped their downtimes. "We need to push ourselves to make it ok in front of the children, keep the worries in the background. It is stressful to lead a song when mums are so tired, but we must keep moving." One mum said, "My energy, some people do not have that. They need to discipline themselves to give to their children!"

The song time with the musician was valued, shown around their song, 'I will carry you.'

The interviewees often referred to the song, and it was a proud flag to fly for refugees and asylum seekers. One said, "We must carry other mums. V has just given birth and could not be here, so let's send her the cathedral video!"

Integration: The opportunities to share African instruments and strum a harp or Ukulele created meaningful ways for the children to join music-making. The performance across the diverse community that also attended binds women together, laughing over songs. Bouncing a child on the adult's lap in one song led to all children being helped by all adults, and often, the children were not with their parents but enjoying confidently mixing with other adults in the group. These were often referred to as "Auntie" by the children and fellow Mothers as "Sister". This was also true across different ethnic groups. The vocal tutor commented on how much she learned from the mothers in the group, "They welcomed me with open arms to this group. In the UK, it doesn't feel like we have the same openness between families; the community these women create and the support they give each other is a valuable lesson for English women to learn."

Leadership: This project built capacity between the participants. The musicians and Carriers of Hope staff worked as music professionals alongside Early Years practitioners in a challenging environment for women with English as a second language. Participation levels were exceptionally high, with 16 -18 families every week. The parents also appreciated the group structure, where different people led the singing, one taking a fuller leadership role than others. (A. said, "One day you will lead the songs!" pointing to a shy parent who had not yet developed her English. It was seen as a 'position' in the group to stand up and clown around, and all the other women appreciated the humour, laughing and flapping their hands at the lead. It was a comical situation that all could laugh at.

Ways of working: The participants need to be responsible and empathetic ways of working. The staff ensured enough food and nappies to enable them to join in without their children being uncomfortable or hungry. The local women had many strengths, bringing their style of music and dance to the sessions, and the staff created an environment that promoted musical agency and attentive listening in the group. At first, women spoke over each other and let their children run around. Still, soon they started to help their children to use an instrument or sit on a lap and listen to the singing, saving their conversation for outside the designated half-hour reserved for singing. These skills would be needed for the stage in the Cathedral. Prioritising participant-led music-making, being culturally responsive and keeping some sort of order was a role all took, including the women themselves, "Listen, mummies, this is a song for your children, please enjoy it." (A). The individuals in the group all needed to have their voices amplified and heard since they were all unique.

Partnerships: The project was a partnership between 2 organisations (Carriers of Hope, Coventry and ExCathdera), an independent practitioner (the composer) and the parents in the group. Collective expertise was harnessed throughout. The experience of Carriers of Hope working with the families over many years helped create an experience that felt well-supported and familiar for the participants. In organising the performance, the concert producer, vocal tutor and group leader worked hard to ensure facilities, timings, rehearsals, resources, and refreshments were appropriate for the families. Communication, collective support, advice, reflection on the group's experiences and encouraged participation in the sessions and the final performance were facilitated via WhatsApp.

Learning: Many parents agreed that the sessions helped them "learn new things for ourselves and our babies."

The project was helping with English as, week-on-week non-English speakers joined in. Even those with English said it helped them "learn the language and how to pronounce things."

The staff and parents noticed some very good musical developments, and observations of the videos showed this clearly. All but two children began to tap percussion instruments with a stronger sense of beat. A lot could jump and turn around without falling over. The use of rhythm sticks (claves), clapping, and stamping demonstrated that children could physicalise the beat, and some had a strong sense of the rhythm of the words of the songs. Singing helped with some rhythm and pitch. One girl of 18 months screamed throughout many sessions, being very sensitive to the noise made by others. By the end, she managed to sit with her mum and grandma, sucking her dummy and focusing on not looking at anybody. This developmental difference may not have been picked up in a usual contact.

Another little girl raced around with instruments in a cart, oblivious to all the sound-making except when staff caught her eye with a song.

The group encouraged the parents to sit their children on their knees or to encourage them to shake an instrument. The group leaders and musicians encouraged the parents to praise their children, but as usual for this age group, many mobile babies just wanted to run. One mother said, "He started to focus. If I said jump, he jumped!" Other parents joined in, saying their child had learnt the words and actions. It was clear that they had observed their toddler exhibiting new behaviours by singing short phrases of a song in unison with the melody, with the remaining notes not in unison with the melody. There was evidence that children were distinguishing between different voices and instruments. Some little ones held onto the musician's knee, hoping to absorb the music and vibrations of the ukulele strings. Many children wanted to get closer to the ukulele to see how it made a sound and to try plucking the strings themselves. At appropriate moments, the musician would encourage the children to strum the ukulele and experiment with the sound their hands could make on the instrument. Mothers talked about how the singing led to music at home and reported having sung the group's composed song, 'I will carry you', at sleep time.

Parents reported that, "Nya loves the bumpy song" and, "I like Twinkle Twinkle, but we don't sing it a lot; we need to sing it more!" Some parents laughed and told about the different bits their child had picked up, "She shouts hooray at bedtime to get me to sing the song!"

The parents learnt the songs and the children learnt parts of songs and actions and in doing so, all learnt English words for lots of things.

We discovered that through experience with different instruments and types of music, children slowly become aware of differences in pitch, timbre, and volume and become increasingly more able to physicalise a steady beat. Even young babies looked surprised when one egg shaker made a different sound from all the others. We enjoyed the children as performers. We enjoyed being together.

In conclusion, what did the parents say:
- The parents want more puppets and instruments.
- More home songs from all women sharing the songs from their own culture.
- The involvement of musicians to lead more of the sessions. "Pippa is so good!"
- More performance opportunities
- More making their songs
- A mix of newer songs and old ones.

Recommendations

The positive outcomes for all the participants described above lead to the following recommendations for policy and practice when creating culturally appropriate early years music experiences.
1. Try to gain increased and sustained access to musicians, especially for families living in asylum-seeking accommodation or refugees whose homes are very poor.
2. Seek support from Migrant support organisations or charities to provide the group's basic needs. We needed more instruments and puppets.
3. Find out about local integration opportunities and places where existing arts are available to refugee and asylum-seeking children.
4. Link-local agencies, community groups, charities, or statutory organisations through targeted partnership funding streams to harness the expertise and co-deliver music.
5. Build inter-agency platforms of exchange between academic and non-academic partners to increase expertise and research opportunities to evaluate such projects.
6. Invest in research alongside developing new initiatives to lead to change and action underpinned by data-driven knowledge. Evidence-based and reflective practice for the organisation ensures the best experience for the asylum seekers and refugees client group and is more likely to result in the initiative's sustainability.
7. Find ways to put the women in charge, so include leadership opportunities for project participants from the planning stage onwards.
8. Provide multiple opportunities for social interaction to build a sense of community and enhance the quality of life for the people living in marginalised communities.
9. Leaders to ensure that every group is empathetic, flexible, and culturally responsive; and is based on the needs and strengths of the participants within the group.

Enable parents to feel more confident to sing with their children at home. Encouraging parents to see the value of singing as a developmental necessity might be particularly important. It is most effective when singing happens one-to-one, face to face with 'serve and return' style interaction with an infant. It would be good to help parents have the confidence to do this without the support of a phone / YouTube/videos. Acapella singing with their children is very simple but very impactful.

8 PRESENTING ONE'S FINDINGS – CREATING AN ORAL PRESENTATION USING RESEARCH METHODS

Part of being an academic is sharing your research; the best way to do this is to gain confidence in presenting in your class or at conferences. Firstly, choose a section of your work that you feel is ready; it may be your methodology chapter or the findings. It must fit the conference's themes; you can find these strands on their websites. Identify your strand on your paper. The presentation can be a poster, PowerPoint, or any other technology you are happy to use. Your supervisor can help you prepare, or you can seek a private tutor like me. To make sure your evidence or literature is up to date, you can use a PRISMA.

To present your research clearly and concisely, you could consider structuring your presentation as follows:

I. Introduction
- Briefly introduce the topic of teaching English as a second language to children in their early years.
- State the purpose of your research and the questions you aim to answer.

II. Methods
- Explain the PRISMA technique you used to conduct your literature search.
- Provide details on the databases, keywords, and inclusion/exclusion criteria you used
- Mention any limitations or potential biases in your search.

III. Results
- Present the findings of your literature search organised around the thematic questions you developed.
- For each question, summarise the main points from the literature and any common themes or disagreements among the sources.
- Avoid making sweeping unsubstantiated claims and focus on what the literature said.
- Cite your sources appropriately.

IV. Conclusion
- Summarise the main findings of your research.
- Discuss any implications or recommendations for teaching children English as a second language in their early years.
- Mention any limitations or gaps in the literature that warrant further research.

The key is to be clear and concise in presenting your research while providing enough detail to support your claims. Headings and subheadings can guide the reader and make it easier to follow your argument. Remember to cite your sources appropriately and avoid overgeneralising or making unsupported claims.

The Technique of Collecting References

The PRISMA technique (Preferred Reporting Items for Systematic Reviews and Meta-Analyses) is a widely recognised and highly regarded for conducting systematic reviews and meta-analyses in healthcare research. The PRISMA technique provides a checklist and flow diagram for authors to use when reporting on systematic reviews and meta-analyses. The PRISMA technique aims to improve the transparency and quality of reporting for systematic reviews and meta-analyses, thereby helping readers assess the validity and reliability of the research findings.

The PRISMA checklist includes 27 items covering a systematic review or meta-analysis's key aspects, including the search strategy, inclusion and exclusion criteria, data extraction, and statistical analysis. In addition, the PRISMA flow diagram provides a visual representation of identifying and selecting studies for inclusion in the review or meta-analysis and the reasons for exclusion.

Overall, the PRISMA technique is a valuable tool for researchers conducting systematic reviews and meta-analyses and for readers who want to appraise such research's quality and reliability critically.

The literature search was explained using PRISMA techniques, and then I themed the search question and findings into questions such as:

- What should be taught in English as a second language for children in their early years?
- Who should teach English to children?
- The literature also cited Where ESL should be taught.

N.B. This could go off into sweeping unsubstantiated claims but should be kept tight to what the literature said and to only three sections.

The objective of helping others to see and criticise your research can only be met if it is clear what you are presenting, so less is better than trying to get a whole chapter in!

Use headings which tells the audience what section of research you will deal with; then the methods of finding your literature, how you logged in with a PRISMA, and then theme your results. Answering certain questions will help you to theme the literature and give a clear conclusion.

The write-up using your literature should include examples from practice so the audience can take time to process what you have to say.

Once the literature was logged into "Mendeley", a reference manager, the abstract and title of each paper were logged onto an Excel sheet to create a catalogue of relevant papers. Then the papers were themed to present the findings for this literature review. The main themes currently are "what to teach" and "how to teach" English as a Second Language (E2L).

The second category of themes was "who should teach E2L "and "where should E2L be taught.

You must include your search terms and methods in any written explanation of your methods. This is an example of a write-up in a thesis. It includes methods, inclusion /exclusion criteria and the PRISMA.

Method

The topic of foreign language education in early childhood was entered into the Web of Science database using a Boolean search https://www.webofscience.com/wos/woscc/basic-search

The search terms were publications (preschool OR early childhood) AND (ESL OR EFL OR second language). This is a BOOLEAN search term using AND, OR and brackets.

The period was from 2017 to the present. Another document type was selected as all types. All outside the chosen dates were excluded.

This first resulted in a total of 22 studies, but 10 were excluded. See figure 1 and 2 for reasons

The paper number on the WOS report	Topic	Exclusion reasons
1	Vaccine report	Wrong topic
4	Early school leavers	Wrong age group
8	Early teacher service leavers	Wrong topic
11	South African inequalities	Wrong topic
13	Older children audience	Wrong age group
15	Homeless children	Wrong topic
17	Beyond primary	Wrong age group
19	Gender and sexual identity	Wrong topic
20	Blood works	Wrong topic
21	Early childhood obesity	Wrong topic

Figure 1

I often present this as a table, but it can be written up. In this study, 10 out of the 22 initially identified studies were excluded based on specific inclusion and exclusion criteria. The following are the reasons for the exclusion:

1. Paper number 1: Vaccine report - This study was excluded as it did not focus on foreign language education in early childhood.
2. Paper number 4: Early school leavers - This study was excluded as it did not focus on the age group of interest, which is early childhood.
3. Paper number 8: Early teacher service leavers - This study was excluded as it did not focus on the topic of interest, foreign language education in early childhood.
4. Paper number 11: South African inequalities - This study was excluded as it did not focus on the topic of interest, foreign language education in early childhood.
5. Paper number 13: Older children audience - This study was excluded as it did not focus on the age group of interest, which is early childhood.
6. Paper number 15: Homeless children - This study was excluded as it did not focus on the topic of interest, foreign language education in early childhood.
7. Paper number 17: Beyond primary - This study was excluded as it did not focus on the age group of interest, which is early childhood.
8. Paper number 19: Gender and sexual identity - This study was excluded as it did not focus on the topic of interest, foreign language education in early childhood.
9. Paper number 20: Blood works - This study was excluded as it did not focus on the topic of interest, foreign language education in early childhood.
10. Paper number 21: Early childhood obesity - This study was excluded as it did not focus on the topic of interest, foreign language education in early childhood.

These explicit inclusion and exclusion criteria ensure that the studies included in the review are relevant to the research question and meet specific quality standards, such as being peer-reviewed and written in English.

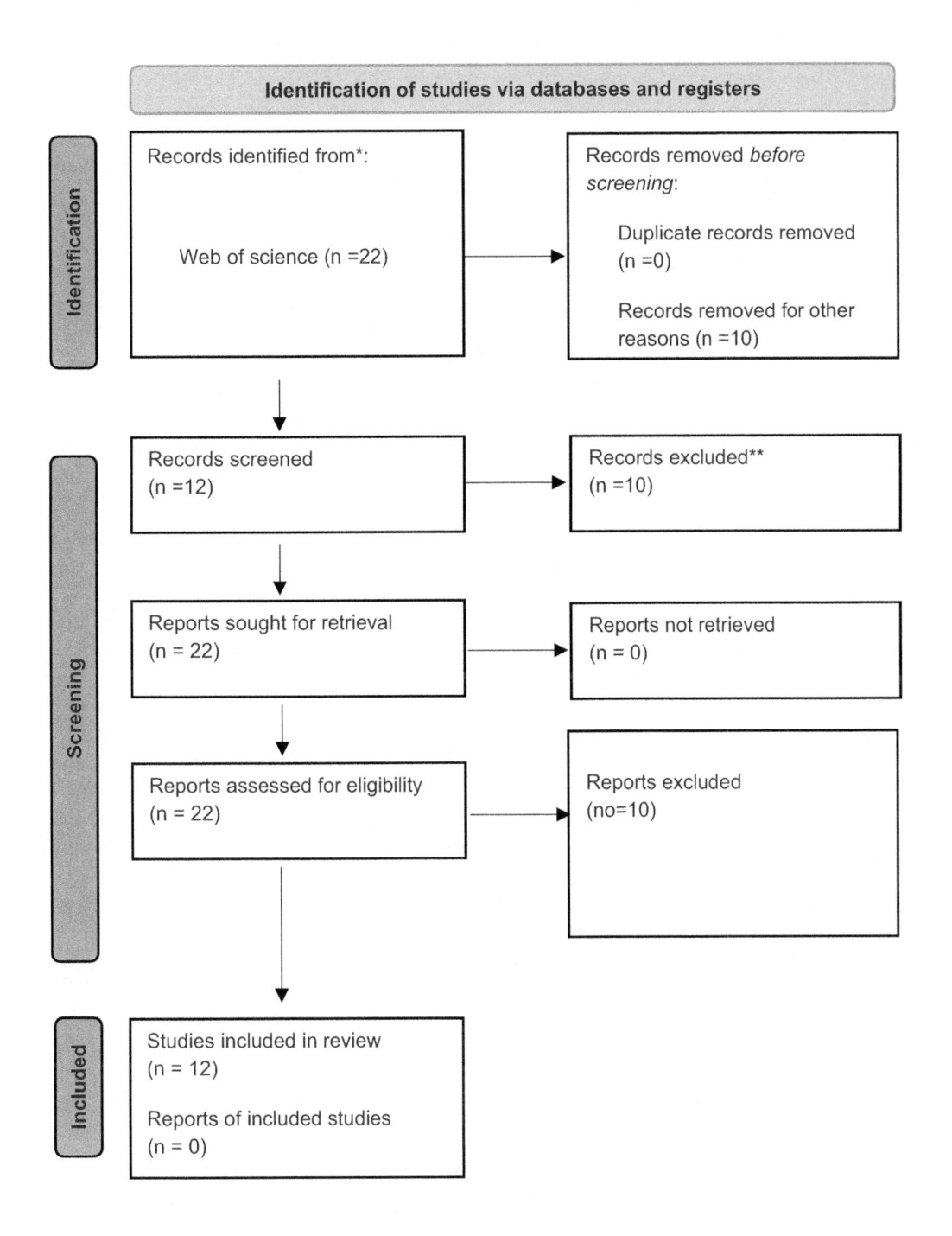

Identification of studies via databases and registers

Identification

Records identified from*:
Web of science (n =22)

Records removed *before screening*:
Duplicate records removed (n =0)
Records removed for other reasons (n =10)

Screening

Records screened (n =12)

Records excluded** (n =10)

Reports sought for retrieval (n = 22)

Reports not retrieved (n = 0)

Reports assessed for eligibility (n = 22)

Reports excluded (no=10)

Included

Studies included in review (n = 12)
Reports of included studies (n = 0)

Figure 2

From: Page MJ, McKenzie JE, Bossuyt PM, Boutron I, Hoffmann TC, Mulrow CD, et al. The PRISMA 2020 statement: an updated guideline for reporting systematic reviews. BMJ 2021;372:n71. doi: 10.1136/BMJ.n71

What to Teach and How

Mudzielwana (2016) suggests that teaching children vocabulary should involve active participation. In his paper, he explains how literature can be effectively taught by utilizing the environment and a structured approach that encourages children to talk more than the teacher. This approach emphasizes the importance of social interactions for English language learners, as it allows them to engage with challenging situations and reach for their academic vocabulary knowledge.

According to constructivist theory, literacy is a social practice, and successful talkers develop their skills through social interactions.

Language Learning Strategies (LLS) refer to learners' methods and techniques to acquire a new language. These strategies can vary from individual to individual and depend on the learner's age, learning style, motivation, and cultural background. Examples of LLS include memorization, inferencing, summarizing, and self-monitoring.

Vocabulary Language Strategies (VLS) specifically focus on acquiring and retaining vocabulary in a new language. VLS can involve various techniques, such as guessing the meaning of a word from context, using visual aids, creating associations, and using repetition and review.

The literature review on the philosophical concept of LLS and VLS is helpful for language teaching and reading researchers at all levels. It provides insight into the different strategies used by language learners and the effectiveness of these strategies. This information can be valuable for educators who want to design effective language teaching programs that cater to the individual needs of their students. Additionally, it can help researchers better understand how learners acquire and retain vocabulary, which can lead to more effective teaching practices.

You might stop here in your presentation and ask for examples from the audience.

Another study examined the use of pronouns among young children. This interests early childhood workers since psychological connections can be made between using me mine pronouns and developing the child's ego. For example, "me goed" is first used, then "I go" The use of "I "is important. (Samad et al. 2016).

However, in a learning English as a Second Language (ESL) situation, the acquisition of pronouns may be influenced by other factors such as exposure to the forms and the student's first language. Samad's study is mainly descriptive, so it is qualitative, and the sample is 5 to 6-year-old Malaysian ESL pre-schoolers. N=40 children.

Methods: The children in the study were presented with 33 drawings to assess their familiarity with subjective, objective, possessive and reflexive English pronouns. For each picture, the children were required to select the correct pronoun from the three pronouns used in a sentence to describe the drawing.

The outcomes were assessed as accuracy rates and errors. This leads to how to teach children English pronouns using child-friendly methods and games.

The study tells us the order in that children use "the boy" or "they", which is helpful for teaching. Finally, the presentation of pronouns to children should also consider groupings that can address specific issues or concerns, as observed in this study. For example, as the students were observed to use names more than pronouns, the introduction of third-person singular pronouns such as he and she should be done in situations where the discourse will include names followed by the relevant pronouns.

Similarly, the specific errors made, such as my one and me instead of I, as indicated by the reports, can be addressed by enhancing the correct forms through oral emphasis or gestures during teacher-led play or demonstration.

A paper by Harris (2019) supports emerging technology to teach young children languages due to its potential as a powerful pedagogical tool.

This research work aims at assessing some factors that facilitate and hinder the sound pedagogical use of ICTs within the context of English as a second language (ESL) at the early childhood education level, using Design Thinking (DT) as a method to define the requirements of great use of emerging technologies in education.

Two ad hoc questionnaires were handed out to school executives and teachers in the specific educational context of Barranquilla, Colombia. The surveys were applied to n=25 preschools.

The qualitative data analysis made with SPSS showed the importance and the need to integrate into the school curriculum technological tools that both improve knowledge and skills and allow for the pedagogical assessment and monitoring of pupils. SPSS stands for Statistical Package for the Social Sciences. It is a software program widely used for statistical analysis in social science research and other fields. SPSS provides various tools and capabilities for data management, transformation, descriptive statistics, visualisation, and advanced statistical analysis. It allows researchers to input data, manipulate variables, perform statistical tests, create charts and graphs, and generate reports.

SPSS offers a user-friendly interface that allows researchers to interact with the software through menus, dialogue boxes, and syntax commands. It supports various statistical techniques, including regression analysis, analysis of variance (ANOVA), factor analysis, cluster analysis, t-tests, chi-square tests, and many others.

The frustrations of low technology or inadequate training to use the available programme were mentioned, yet this writer pushed ahead to declare augmented reality as the way to go in education. Not without infrastructure and support to design concepts using proper pedagogy …maybe he is selling the idea without evidence, I think so.

The next paper chosen to present from this search about **how to teach** is Van Rhyn, and Van Staden, (2018)

Their study emphasised early intervention of ESL so children can enjoy later school subjects in English.

Their sample is pre-schoolers with whom they do a baseline test to prove they have poor literacy before they start to learn at school. The methodology included a baseline test and results of several literacy surveys and tests, which demonstrated that their learners' literacy abilities are far below standard, even in their mother tongue and were very weak compared to cohorts in other international countries. Following a quasi-experimental pre-test/post-test research design, ESL learners (N = 85) were purposively drawn from schools in the Gauteng Province of South Africa to participate in this study.

The study insists that technology is the way forward based on their excellent results that determine the value of interactive storybook reading as an intervention strategy to support the reading comprehension of ESL learners.

Would the children have improved as much with any intervention or was the attraction of using a computer a big incentive to practice and remember??

Who Should Teach English as a Second Language? (ESL)

A dearth of literature suggests parents should be taught English so they can practice speaking with their child and give weight to learning a second language.

A paper by Van Rhyn (2018) focuses on the inequalities in South Africa's education system, especially for the early years pupils who are learning a second language ESL at school The study focuses on challenges for Early years teachers when creating responsive literacy environments for young learners. By reviewing the literacy assessment outcomes. Van Rhyn evidence that the South African education system fails to address the literacy needs of many South African learners.

Van Rhyn 's study employed a qualitative, interpretive research design, interviewing 30 teacher participants from urban and rural South African schools to determine the daily challenges they experience in teaching literacy to young learners. There is an appetite to teach English to all children very early on, but parents must be on board with the teaching.

Sommer et al. (2020) also proposed innovative ways of teaching ESL They also involved immigrant parents and children, in their case, Latinos in the USA. A closer inspection shows that some parents dropped out of the Headstart5 programme, so their results are based on nearly half (46%) of the parents who completed two semesters, so 18 parents, in the end.

This mixed-methods study explores the progress and the perspectives of parents and staff in this ESL program over two semesters (n = 35). Among enrollees in each semester, parents had high levels of completion (83% in semester 1; 70% in semester 2) and class attendance (94% in semester 1; 88% in semester 2).

They used a robust measure of the National Reporting Systems and evidenced some movement in English language skills, moving on average from beginner to high intermediate levels. There was also a focus group where parents and staff discussed why involving the family in the child's ESL was best.

A complaint about this paper is that they did not deal with the normal living conditions of parents and families and why parents dropped out. Was the curriculum alien to the parents? Were they anxious? Did they have to attend work? Care for other children?

Williams, and Lowrance-Faulhaber, (2018) also concluded that parents and family languages should be important when teaching young children a second language. This research paper agrees with most that writing is important for academic achievement, but more research needs to examine writing in bilingual students, particularly in early childhood. So, they try to fill this gap in the research by carrying out a literature review focusing on writing with young bilingual children.

The methodology: A search of databases for studies published between 2000 and 2017 yielded 35 peer-reviewed articles that met inclusion criteria.

The findings from a content analysis demonstrated that young bilingual children develop knowledge and understanding of print and a range of composing strategies that support bilingual and bi-literate writing.

However, the most interesting part of teaching bi-lingual children was that authentic activities are better than direct teaching, which isolates chalk-and-talk strategies that are less effective than meaning-based learning, which is contextualised within authentic activities and creates curricular space for multimodal forms of literacy.

Laso Genre-based writing instruction, technology-mediated composing, and ESL-enhanced content area literacy instruction also was found to be supportive.

The evidence indicated that instruction in the native language and dual language instruction supported biliteracy. Both languages should be used, indicating a need to involve the family languages.

There is a move towards using technology in language teaching, and this may lead to teaching by rote or pressing the buttons whilst the child sits alone to get a language response that the child must copy. Practitioners might use this as a time filler, but obviously, it is a poor language teacher if it doesn't invoke some of the child's interaction, higher-order thinking questions, cognitive abilities, and multi-sensory needs to learn. There is always the argument that technology is a big investment for schools, nurseries, and family homes. However, the following paper by Chen et al. (2021) encourages early years workers to design their curriculum around using the technology available in the environment they work in,

Some studies highlight parental anxiety around teaching ESL Chen et al (2021) Chen and Wen, (2021). To relieve children of some stress, the Chinese Ministry of Education implemented an Early Education policy that forbids formal literacy (e.g., Chinese character recognition and Pinyin) and more ambitious literacy teaching practices (e.g., Teaching English as a second language) in kindergartens.

Yet parents all over the world can see the value of education; indeed, most rely on classroom education to be an equaliser for their children. They want to get their child further ahead by helping with the teaching. The research has gaps identified in this paper that we need to learn about the relationship between parental aspirations and their willingness to read at home. (e.g., shared book reading) in poorer homes with less-educated families in China.

This study intends to address this dearth in the literature by applying structural equation modelling to a sample of 4395 middle to low-SES parents in China. The findings show that, contrary to the policy makers' expectation that downplaying Chinese word recognition and ESL would encourage information literacy practices, highly anxious Chinese parents are motivated by their children's Chinese word recognition to engage in shared book reading with their children. Without this motivator, highly anxious parents would read to their children even less. Calm parents were more likely to be motivated by their children's new English learning.

Many English language teachers and classroom teachers know they should work together on the early-year curriculum, according to Hsieh and Teo (2021.)

Using a methodology of observations and interviews, this study examined seven Taiwanese ECTs' perspectives on and experiences of collaborative teaching with ELTs and analysed the factors influencing this collaboration. The results showed that most participants collaborated minimally with ELTs and usually followed a "one teach, one assist" approach.

Organisational, interpersonal, and personal factors affected collaboration. Specifically, this study's findings suggest that traditional Chinese values, emphasising harmony, may prevent ECTs from offering advice, co-planning curricula, or sharing their expertise with ELTs. Although most ECTs performed secondary roles and viewed English lessons as a break from their duties, they acknowledged their contribution to children's education. Finally, an individual case revealed that raising teachers' pedagogical awareness led to greater engagement in English instruction.

Pre-service teachers' perception is of interest to this field, and one particularly well-researched paper is by Lo, Goswami, and Inoue (2010).

This study investigated pre-service teachers' perceptions toward instructional strategies regarding English language Learners (ELL). Research has suggested that teachers with an adequate understanding of effective instructional strategies for LCD students are likelier to engage in appropriate instruction and facilitate learning. The methodology was to use a survey of n=129. Another qualitative study Stage two was subsequently, semi-structured individual interviews were conducted with 12 participants. The quantitative data were analysed with descriptive and inferential statistics; the qualitative data were analysed with theory-based themes.

Results in the study found that participants, in general, were willing to encourage interaction between students; include students' home culture in the classroom; promote students' native; hold high expectations; incorporate students' native in instruction; ask higher-order thinking questions; conduct a student-centred classroom; use activities to facilitate interaction; access students' prior knowledge through instructional conversation; provide visuals and nonverbal cues; scaffold students' learning; and finally, utilise hands-on activities.

To conclude this systematic literature review, twelve papers were found with one search on the Web of Science. In answer to "*what*" should be taught and how vocabulary and pre-fixes are receiving attention in the research as the main content for teaching English. The teaching and learning research suggests a play approach that employed meta-cognitive processes over teaching words off the board. The early years research shows that teaching and learning should be led by children, preferably through technology and not set by teachers.

The "*who*" should teach shows that partnerships between parents and different professionals should be built and treasured. Parents' home language should be used alongside English. However, this is difficult for nervous parents and busy parents. Professionals found that including children and their parents is challenging due to how organisations are set up and interpersonal factors between the staff.

Schools treated staff teaching English as an add-on, not a main partnership. All agree English should be taught to children early, but a check on whether they have skills in their mother tongue first is useful.

9 PREPARING A SYNOPSIS

My good friend Professor David Stuckler introduced me to the notion that there is an order to present the research you have carried out. First, he referenced Aristotle's secret to the perfect presentation. The stages are Pathos, where you use a notion to grip the audience. The introduction to this presentation opened the hearts and minds of my conference attendees. It started by talking about Fatima and described her life as a refugee seeking education and a future in the UK.

Next, Aristotle, and David, suggest "Ethos". This section identifies for the audience why you should listen to me. I put forward my work as an educator with a very marginalised group -the refugees in Coventry. Lastly comes the "Logos" or the logic. This is the meat or the content of the research. Using this method, I have an interesting talk that doesn't go on and on without point. I can return to Fatima at the end of the presentation, considering what research said about the educational outcomes for groups such as this.

The conference often asks for a synopsis.

Educating Fatima and her sisters: a report of refugee women and their Participation in education in Coventry UK

A presentation and paper to be considered for the I.C.E.Q 2020.

Abstract

The presentation focuses on how women use education to cope with the forced situation of being displaced as a refugee and considers the agency of these women and the strength of education to create new beginnings.

An important finding in this venture was the strength of women asylum seekers and refugees to attend and achieve education modules even though they had separated from their homes and were stopped from joining mainstream adult education in the UK. Asylum seekers need access to public funds or education. Their status prevents them from legal, social and economic structures as refugees in the UK.

Women who are withdrawn from society and experiencing negative emotions such as depression, loneliness, and hopelessness usually cannot do well in education. They are vulnerable to layers of being a woman, displaced, with recent experiences of death and war. The academic term for this is "liminality" Liminality is a term used to describe the psychological process of transitioning across boundaries and borders. The term "limen" comes from the Latin for threshold; it is the threshold separating one space from another.

This study presents how the women used the educational situation to help them to cope and adapt and to reframe their existence in a foreign situation.

The general result was that the women gained soft skills such as social graces, communication abilities, language skills, personal awareness, cognitive or emotional empathy, time management, teamwork and leadership traits.

And gained greater self-awareness and strength and regained agency over their lives by using the "waiting time" between getting here and gaining the right to remain, to learn.

IN THEIR OWN WORDS

10 EDUCATING FATIMA AND HER SISTERS

Abstract
What are the current thoughts on education for all?
Quality in education has come to mean inclusion, diversity, and equal opportunities. My name is Dr. Lin Armstrong and I work with Coventry University and Warwick University. I also work with refugees and asylum-seeking women in Coventry with a charity called "Carriers of Hope". I am the link between the universities and the women. This is a reflective account of this work.

This chapter focuses on how women use education to cope with the forced situation of being displaced as a refugee and considers the agency of these women and the strength of education to create new beginnings. Inclusion is when all learners have their education designed to suit them. They reach praxis *Pedagogy of the Oppressed.* (Freire 1970).

Rancier (1987) considered how education in universities was considered to be just for very clever people with good families and the academics consider themselves better than the students.

Rancière's book, *The Ignorant Schoolmaster: Five Lessons in Intellectual Emancipation* (original title *Le Maître ignorant: Cinq leçons sur l'émancipation intellectuelle*, published in 1987) was written for educators and educators-to-be. Through the story of Joseph Jacotot, Rancière challenges his readers to consider equality as a starting point rather than a destination. In doing so, he asks educators to abandon the themes and rhetoric of cultural deficiency and salvation. Rather than requiring informed schoolmasters to guide students towards prescribed and alienating ends, Rancière argues that educators can channel equal intelligence in all to facilitate their intellectual growth in virtually unlimited directions. The schoolmaster need not know anything (and maybe ignorant). Rancière begins with the premise that all are of equal intelligence and that any collective educational exercise founded on this principle can provide the insights from which knowledge is constructed. He claims that the poor and disenfranchised should feel perfectly able to teach *themselves* whatever it is they want to know. Furthermore, anyone can lead, and the oppressed should not feel bound to experts or reliant on others for their intellectual emancipation.

There are challenges in offering educational projects to refugees in the UK including the exclusion due to social policy -no educational facilities can take refugees on until they have the right to remain which could take years in the UK? The informal education offered by this charity have other limitations and challenges. The women have no paper pens computers and they have tiny children to care for. There is also fact that English is their additional language and many do not have more than a basic awareness of the language, all education is taught in English in this case study. The women also have a struggle with poverty and the call to asylum meetings or medical meetings may mean their money is taken up so they do not have Bus fares to training centers nor phone credit to join online sessions. Having explained who the learner is, women with a lack of belief in life and low esteem this work now goes onto discuss what is being masked about education provision and displaced people, labeling and judging in education for adults. The politicians are not the only ones to blame our schools and universities should be open for all and they have unachievable entrance thresholds and fees. I argue we must not blame the victims, the refugees, but accommodate their predicament and solving a problem in education: education for women who are excluded in society.

First published in Portuguese in 1968, Pedagogy of the Oppressed was translated and published in English in 1970. Paulo Freire's work has helped to empower countless people throughout the world and can now be used to analyse the way women refugees are being limited in progressing in their life.

Working with a charity Carriers of Hope an inclusive model of education developed before COVID-19 2020-2021 and is still going. Critical pedagogy is when we discuss what is education and who is it for. It allows for the views of the learners and inspires learners and gives them freedom. The banking concept, (Freire 1970), is how the teaching is viewed as filling up learner's heads with middle-class views. Education is typically taught by the middle class and the subject content is based on the view of those educators. This negates the experiences and strengths of women who are often seen as an underclass among the other underprivileged and minorities in cities and urban centers. This is ongoing unless some part of the system alters, the way of accepting women into education. For the most part "Carriers of Hope" used my skills to train women in all sorts of childcare and care work and the unique offer helped the women to go onto more formal education with standardised certificates. The education set them up for further training once they had their letter saying they have a right to stay in the UK. Some went on to Coventry University, some went into community education, and some were well prepared to volunteer in nurseries and care homes. Many learned English and how the school systems work to help their children in education. The fact that so many could use their fundamental intelligence to make connections in the host community lead to power and a chance to say what is going on for their families.

The modules designed were designed to match the standards used in teaching childcare and care in the UK. The sessions were open to anyone with refugee or asylum-seeking status and attendance offered several benefits for non-English speakers :

Concepts and laws about care are introduced again and again

Agencies that can help children are introduced again and again

Women help others by translating in class

Information, videos, and contacts are shared on WhatsApp.

Women teach others how to use their phones to get free entry into places and to gain news of work.

They also share their lessons and videos about knowledge building up knowledge as in connectivism. (Downes 2009)

The modules taught for vocations in care and childcare.

The volunteers ask for help to fill in university and college applications. They also get assistance in creating a CV ready for work.

Each module has a section where the language used for that vocation can be learned.

Women with little children come to feel they are working towards when they can work

All modules are designed to match university modules

Children's health and education

The modules were evaluated using a simple google doc form and a translator from the group. Later Coventry University put on a Citizens social science course with certification that taught the women research and furthered their English skills. It was obvious the benefits were social to improve mental healthy and educational to improve the future opportunities to settle in the community workforce.

Feedback from women was so positive many, many more joined the sessions.

Before we were always in our refuge rooms- even to talk to others was not as it is now,

Now we are discussing and learning from each other so am happy and appreciate it.

Thank you so much Carriers of Hope for helping us out! We appreciate the efforts of our volunteers who make such an event possible and successful.

It has been a lot of work, but you have done such a good job!

The only way to become smarter, better, happier, livelier and wiser, is to help others, just like you have!

The sessions are very Educational to us as mothers and they also reduce a lot of stress or panic because a lot of things are explained. The kids also enjoy interacting with others and it's good for their mental growth as well.

I am exposed to different parental skills that I did not possess previously. The sessions keep us occupied, improve our social skills and thus help to reduce our stress levels. I am also grateful to Dr. Lin who teaches us English as the people in the refuge that she is helping started to communicate in English with confidence, which is great.

Women who are withdrawn from society and experiencing negative emotions such as depression, loneliness, hopelessness usually cannot do well in education. They are vulnerable to layers of being a woman, displaced, with recent experiences of death and war. The academic term for this is "liminality" Liminality is a term used to describe the psychological process of transitioning across boundaries and borders. The term "limen" comes from the Latin for threshold; it is literally the threshold separating one space from another.

An important finding in this venture was the strength of women asylum seekers and refugees to attend and achieve modules of education even though they had separated from their homes and were stopped from joining in mainstream adult education in the UK. Asylum seekers cannot access public funds nor education. Their status prevented them from legal, social, and economic structures refugees in the UK

Another unseen outcome was the sessions were linked to helping the children to learn and develop but the parents became adult educators as well. Veena posted lots of links to songs on the web whilst working through her music module. Other parents got help from her to complete their modules.

The women completing all the childcare modules became volunteers for the creches to put more training on. Volunteers taught other volunteers or looked after the children whilst a session was going on in the church. Children played whilst their mums discussed differences and similarities between countries and childcare and education systems.

The growth of technology skills proved invaluable during the COVID-19 lockdown. The development from the sessions was as unique as the training. It allowed for personal growth and networking. Help is available when the women work at home so many requested a computer from the charity and worked hard to learn IT skills. When the first women became more proficient they setup their Zoom meetings during lockdown to encourage each other by showing videos of their children learning to cook or paint or play. The housing of refugees and asylum seekers is very poor so, this raised spirits in a time where it would be easy to be isolated and depressed.

After the lockdown, the strong bonds continued. The women made "WhatsApp" groups to share learning and useful finds like free trips. They arranged meet-ups in parks and brought food to share. The recreation of an extended family helped the children to find playmates when starting a new class.

There was a good atmosphere in the sessions and friends were made by sharing their own experiences of childbirth and pregnancy. They reported cases of racism and poor service. They could be there for new women at the beginning of their asylum-seeking journey.

Education also helped the lone women to make sense of the differences between their culture and the host culture and I found there are many differences in how mums help their children to learn social behavior. In the UK there is no smacking when you are a childcare worker yet many women relied on physical discipline at first. Notes are made in both languages and I hope to create a multi-lingual Understanding of children's behaviors.

In conclusion, Ranciere argued that people are perfectly capable of learning for themselves without the intervention of the usual skilled pedagogy. Indeed the learners would learn what they need even if the pedagogues themselves knew nothing about the subject or what they needed to transform their knowledge to useful knowledge to relocate to the UK. This proves, just as Ranciere said there is a fundamental equality of intelligence amongst human beings even if they are labeled " women refugees" without any station in society.

In addition, knowledge was developed in the direction the women needed to live in the host country by a process of linking the new to what was known already.

Conventional models of education in the UK insist people should be clever enough and accomplished enough to attend adult education in university and the tutors are skilled to present what is needed sequentially and progressively. The sessions in this paper were developed with the women themselves picking what was of interest and changing the content to include their world view of the topic. Tutors in universities are paid and expected to produce permanent hierarchical relations between teacher and taught, because " the ignorant can never catch up and bridge the gap between themselves and their teachers "(Ranciere.) This work shows the design of the sessions can teach the ignorant teacher a lot about other world views and reservoirs of knowledge.

11 WRITING REFLECTIVE ACCOUNTS

Some pieces of coursework still require you to use reading to reflect on what you did. It can turn into a magazine article, That you do not want, if you only use descriptive, entertaining writing so do your literature search first. The literature you read will create the headings that you might wish to write under.

Writing a good reflective and academic account of "Learning English Through Play" requires the writer to organise their thoughts, reflect on their learning experiences, and use academic language to communicate ideas effectively. Here are some steps to be followed:

Write a clear and concise introduction that explains what you will be discussing in your reflective and academic account. You can start by providing some context for your learning experience and explaining why you chose to write about learning English through play.

Use academic language to describe your learning experiences and reflect on what you have learned. Use examples and specific details to support your ideas.

Include a conclusion that summarises your main points and reflects on your overall learning experience. Consider discussing how English skills have improved because of playing games and engaging in other play activities.

Review your writing carefully to ensure that it is well-organised, easy to understand, and free of errors.

Remember that the key to writing a good reflective and academic account is, to be honest, clear, and reflective. By following these steps, you can create a well-written and engaging account of your experience learning English through play.

Learning English Through Play for pre-schoolers.

A colleague of mine in the Carriers of Hope charity asked if I had a qualification in Teaching English as a Second Language. (TE2L) or (E2L) I do have several, but do we need one to be a good practitioner in the Early Years? I believe all early year's practitioners can relate to this question where ever they operate in whatever country they work in. The teaching of language to English babies is second nature for practitioners because they are trained for it but are they trained for teaching English as a second or third language?

There may be valuable missing information that needs to be talked about and inserted into early years conferences and courses in every module dealing with English as an additional language.

This chapter hopes to discuss the peculiarities of the children who need to learn English alongside their own language using the principles of informal education and funds of knowledge where the learners bring their own history and culture to the play session. Hedges, H., Cullen, J. and Jordan, B., 2011. Early years curriculum: Funds of knowledge as a conceptual framework for children's interests. Journal of Curriculum Studies, 43(2), pp.185-205.

This is a reflective account of my work with children and their mothers, refugees in Coventry, UK. It highlights the quality of teaching that early year's workers give to English language learners and offers an opportunity for the reader to compare it to early years work they have witnessed. The group for this case study discussion is always called "Lets Play" whether it is held in a refuge, a hotel or a church.

Didactics is a teaching method that ensures quality teaching but in the UK, we also call it pedagogy. Pedagogy considers the teacher, the learner and the class content triad. It is a central theme of English as a second language course. (ESL). It has 4 main areas: approach, methods, procedures, and techniques. These are the usual headings on a teaching and learning plan so are useful to separate and discuss when considering quality outcomes for children who are learning English. One of the most useful things about learning language through play in a refugee playgroup is that all the family can come and help to contextualise that week's theme or subjects and therefore all the family become teachers and learners.

Approach

The approach for many early years workers is based on how we assume language learning takes place. In the UK, as in other countries, language and how it is learned is based on theory. It can be assumed that all early years practitioners have studied the language development of children and carried out and analysed observations on individual children. No matter what level of course taken the early childhood students all start with Chomsky (2000) and perhaps Pinker (1995). The notion that young children find it easy to learn languages because they have a language acquisition device is usual in the UK as in other countries. There are later contributions to linguistic theory such as Hakuta et al,(2003) and Hyltenstam (2001) but the teaching still focuses on Vygotsky (1934) who claims the child will improve their language capabilities by socialising. The innate biological system theory argues that children just need to hear the language and very little teaching is required. The main theory remains that under fives developmental stages is seen as an opportunity to provide multiple learning experiences before the brain loses its plasticity. (Katrakoc 2007) This may be the reason so many children are left to 'get on with it" because learning English is believed to be natural. The quality of adult communication can be an issue in many settings and homes and this is recognised by the government's latest campaign to get babies talking, however, it doesn't recognise second language speakers and they are separated from central messages about language development as if English is the only language necessary.

Human infants are designed to pay attention to the human voice, they are alert to speech and can imitate it according to Murray and Andrews (2000). In the UK studies such as The Social Baby (2004) and Siren films "The Wonder Years (2008) are used to train early years workers to notice the clear evidence that babies are very responsive, and so the quality of adult communication really matters. This shapes all approaches to teaching English as an additional language -we bathe the children in language. Most trained practitioners understand the notion that children listen before they start speaking ((Verdugo & Belmonte, 2007). The more children learn English in a meaningful context the better their second language learning develops (Becker & Roos, 2016;)

In "Let's Play" we have different adults who can sing lullabies in mother tounges and we have created a recording so other parents can hear them on the "Whats app "group for "Let's Play. In this way, we value all languages and do not just promote English. It is a monoglossic approach when just one language is used and this ignores the knowledge and culture a child may already have.

By one-year babies have lost the ability to make sounds that are not in the languages that they hear around them. The tuneful babble of children includes the sound patterns of the languages that they hear. "Let's Play" accounts for this by having a daily circle time for song singing in all languages led by the parents. It has been observed that the innate pre-disposition theory where all children's language development can be set and predicted is challenged since language learning follows a different pattern for each child and family. Some have a Coventry accent when they speak to us and their own language and accent speaking to their family. One little girl said she did not speak Arabic only English. One little boy at three has already learnt to speak English to me and Arabic to his mum. I am learning Arabic and wish to practice with him but he is having none of it!

Continuing with language theory that is commonly taught in adult education, Skinner (date) is used to theorise that parents reward correct versions of the language used but do not reward mistakes. The idea in "Lets Play" is the language that is correct gets rewarded. Building on familiar words like "tidy up time" every play session but nothing is frowned upon because this would inhibit a young child's communication, so all tries at communication are rewarded. Rewards and consequences as in conditioning a child cannot be the best explanation of aspects of language development. Early years workers may turn to teaching a child using flash cards and rewards to speak English words without any context but when teaching second languages this is frowned upon. Labelling words in a picture book is the usual way to start assessing English yet responding to instructions like "brush your hair or "brush your shoes " might be a better assessment of receptive language that comes before making the language work in sentences.

Research from neuroscience supports aspects of brain-based, innate theory-human infants tune into spoken language and hearing and vision. Furthermore, parts of the brain can be seen working before birth. The small electrical charges in the brain are tracked by computer imaging to give feedback about a baby's brain. The babies do know their mother's voice and often respond better to adults who speak their language and look like their mothers. This is a consideration in an all-white staff group in a nursery but in "Let's Play" we always have volunteers from the community working alongside us. No theory offers a full explanation of how young children gain language but it is accepted that key adults in their environment have a role to play. It is clear that approaches to teaching English have changed over the years as the research grows and this theory should be included in Early years and teaching courses, not as an add-on or one day but throughout the modules at university.

Method

Methods of teaching English should fit the group or individual we are teaching. Early years practitioners see their role in teaching reading, writing and speaking clearly as following the curriculum. How many have seen the curriculum for second language speaking found here? How to expect language development at each individual child's age and stage is provided for the English children so we do need more research and theory about second or third language speakers.

A notable method in the research evidence is to teach the parent so they can join in with the child. Carriers of Hope do not provide English-speaking classes since they are in the community however Academic Advantage, my own company wanted to provide evening classes to boost the parents' ability to join in classes from home. A report about this is yet to come but it's important to consider what exactly is needed in a class for adults. None of the methods are right or wrong but are chosen for the purpose of learning English. For example, in the adult groups that wanted to learn to write in English, I spoke about grammar, translated, and memorised English in situations such as at the party for Eid. Vygotsky's constructive approach to learning language has received a lot of attention in the early years profession at all levels. This is because his research uses a powerful tool of discursive interaction between the children and other children and the adults.

Techniques

These are the ways used to teach such as question and answer or using the laptop to play stories and rhymes. Techniques are about practices and behaviours according to a particular method. The steps that lead to a particular outcome. The theory of techniques comes in the university modules about learning theory but should also include information about funds of knowledge a child may have.

In "Let's Play" I saw pictures of planes and bombs and what I thought was a lovely sunset -it was the suffocating smoke all around the child's home. We don't know anything about a child's home life until they depict it, yet we design play sessions fit for safe English children discouraging gun play and gun making, ignoring strong feelings and stories.

The parents want to depict safe places for their children so how can early years workers play to give this opportunity? A fishing net and fish that have a safe pond really interested one little boy. He played getting them and them hiding over and over. We taught feeling words with a context, with a play situation and with real feelings. The tent was used as a chase and hide game for three four-year-olds. The same feelings of fear and excitement were acted out and named. The story later had some puppets that were sad and happy. The usual early years play was used to teach English, taking us much further than question and answer with flash cards in circle time. It can also be much more effective than drilling the children. Drilling is a teaching technique where the students learn information in sets like times tables or through repetition of materials. It is a main central technique of ALM (Freeman, 2000: 48) This is seen as necessary to improve intonation and grammar learning according to sites such as https://jobs.languagelink.ru/tefl_clinic/practical_teaching/drilling/. On the positive side, It enables the teacher to make corrections and keep the students' assessments up to date.

One of the disadvantages of drilling is that the context is not taught so the students may memorise but not know a deeper understanding or meaning of the word. There will be some students who cannot keep up the pace so different drilling methods would need to be designed for differentiation. according to https://www.teflcourse.net/blog/drilling-as-a-teaching-method-pros-and-cons/.

Procedures

Harmer (2001) when speaking about E2L identifies a deductive and inductive method that I have seen used in The Montessori teaching methods amongst other theories. A common method used in adult classes is to teach the rule first and then to put it into a sentence. So rules, examples, practice and correction. The opposite is to give the example of the context first. Procedures are informed by methods and of course, suit the practitioner in his or her style.

Naturally, early years workers change their procedures in response to the learners' abilities and this elective approach is expected of the experienced practitioner. However, with children, there is no need to teach formal grammar. It is caught through experiences and use. It is practised in play and then used without even knowing it's a rule of grammar. We know the rule has been learnt from erroneous errors such as "I goed" instead of I went. There is no need to correct these errors but see them as a step in language learning. That will be ironed out when the practitioner provides well-designed play.

Communicative language speaking is the main outcome for the "Let's Play "groups. The methods vary but a good example is when we present a topic for the session, eg; parts of the body or little creatures, all of the usual early year's work. We bring in something to contextualise the subject of the day like a snail in a jar, a storybook about small creatures and some floor mats so we can wriggle like a caterpillar. We have pictures to make and songs to sing so appealingly to small children's fun side to learn the language. We have a silent video about a creepy crawly that children can talk over about the things they see. All usual pre-school language development. The difference is that children's confidence and self-esteem can be raised because the story is explained in their own language. The parents tell of creatures they see as a child and how they feared the hairy critters. The cultural context helps the children to enjoy language learning. This cannot be done in usual groups because most of the practitioners just speak one language, or the second language speakers are sent off with "their" children to teach "them" in another corridor.

In comparison to a country such as Morocco, that has not got a monologic approach, the teachers are competent in different languages and children learn Arabic, French and English the learning of English is easier. They teach English by connecting English in maths classes and other subjects to their mother tongue. In UK research and policy there was a suggestion that practitioners should learn a few words in the child's language to help to settle them into settings. There was also a time when only English could be used in class to force foreigners to speak and learn in English. These policies have shaped our notions of teaching English as a second language but what if we had proper language teaching and the staff to make the nurseries multi-lingual?

Across the world, English is taught in a standard-based approach, a statement of what the learner should know and how they should be able to use English at every level.

Perhaps what is missing from Early years education is the theory of teaching English as a second language so we can pick and choose between them as we do with informal language teaching.

Deductive v Inductive Approach

In all the above examples it can be seen that early years mostly use informal learning and if they do teach by rote -such as colours it is periphery not central to their methods. Widodo (2006) called the deductive approach "rule-driven learning". The grammar rule such as add 'ed' to make a past tense for work (worked) or jump (jumped). The rule is given, and then the examples of sentences are presented by the teacher. Once learners understand the rules, they are told to apply the rules given to various examples of sentences. The disadvantage of this approach according to Michael Swan (cited in Thornbury, 1999, p. 32) is that this method may be off-putting for younger learners and they may not understand the concepts. It is confusing if the children get irregular verbs like swim (swimmed is wrong). It is using teacher transmission which hinders learner involvement and interaction. It is easily forgotten. The deductive approach encourages the belief that learning a language is simply knowing the rules.

Felder and Henriques (1995) stated an inductive approach comes from inductive reasoning. Reasoning progresses from taking part in a language and observing. This then develops into the learner exploring and learning through experiences generalising them to learn general principles and concepts. In short, when we use induction, we observe a number of specific instances and from them infer a general principle or concept. The practitioner would then plan so the instances to learn the language's rules would be increased. This probably happens informally but an informed practitioner could make it so much better.

TPR

Another theory of language learning is TPR. TPR stands for Total Physical Response and was created by Dr. James J Asher. It has three stages and is worth knowing what stage you are at with the individual child. When TPR is applied in the classroom, a teacher is required to provide a model. The model has three vital features: 1) grasping the spoken language must come prior to speaking, 2) comprehension is developed through body movement, and 3) the period of listening period helps a learner to be ready to speak. Such a model does not force the learner to speak. It is also recommended that TPR be applied for only short periods of time because the learner will get tired of doing it.

Early years practitioners do use movement as a memory enhancer, but could this be honed to ensure the second language speakers understand the commands to direct them? The songs such as "heads, shoulder, knees and toes" are used to develop vocabulary. Often we remark on how quickly the children learn English by observing their behaviour. The children come to sit on the mat for a story but really, they are just following the other children who are placed there by their parents. So making the same sign with the same words may help the children to learn to "sit on the mat please" -the meaning of words is comprehended through actions. I think every group does this but more could be learnt about why we do it and if wriggling like a worm increases understanding of a concept.

TPR is based on the way children learn their mother tongue. Parents have "language-body conversations" when they instruct their children. The parent says, "Look at mummy" or "Give me the ball" and the child does so. These conversations continue for many months before the child starts to speak. Even though she can't speak during this time, the child is taking in all of the languages; the sounds and the patterns. Eventually, when she has decoded enough, the child reproduces the language quite spontaneously. TPR attempts to mirror this effect in the language classroom; movements are used for more than vocabulary building.

This method could make adults feel embarrassed as they act out and it could be boring if overused but in the early years, we must take note of the receptive language of each individual child. Rather than assess the child as not being able to speak English we could give opportunities for receptive language once the child has some vocabulary in English.

Cultural Heritage

The principles are is the language fit for inside and outside the session of teaching English? The experience must consider genuine multicultural efforts. The notion that the pictures and artefacts used must be recognisable to the child will mean the practitioner will have to do research or be paired with an adult from that country. There is a fear of tokenism when we don't really know about other countries, but early years practitioners are not just teaching language but exploring learning experiences that can be taken into real-life situations. John Dewey cited in Miettinen, (2000) called this "the new type of education" but it is just good education. It might feel useless showing a chapati roller or tagine to four-year-olds who have never seen them used but does it feel as bad showing the minority children a whole range of English tools for the kitchen? Ideal integration is when my child can name another child's kitchen utensils and vice versa.

The usual activity during September is getting the children ready for school. Getting ready for school sessions is particularly valuable if they are not just one-sided using books from English classrooms but discussing what goes on in education in other places. In some countries children sit behind desks and use the same book to fill in the pages, their education is formal. The children may travel to school by car or walk over mountains to get to a single classroom with all ages of children. In UK schools the advice is to get your child independent in dressing and undressing whilst, in other places, there is a need to learn all the letters of the alphabet. It is easy to consider the refugee child is going to be behind their classmates, another wonderful piece of research to do!

In one "Let's Play" we were focused on shopping and buying food. The three-year-old child wrote his name on the list and proceeded to spell lots of fruit and vegetables in English! He could read!! His mother had taught him at home, so he was not behind in UK schools. The value placed on play in UK groups is not always the same in other countries. There is more teaching by rote in some schools and parents do not see the value of play, so it's usually taught by the practitioners to the parents, and they need to ask parents how it was education carried out in their country. Even if children are born in the UK, they will have influences from their parent's own education.

Using Expressions

It is accepted in education that the sign of quality in learning is the teacher's talking time is low and the learner's time to talk is very high. Yet in English language learning many practitioners feel the need to give vocabulary for the child to copy repeatedly. In the hope to get English up to scratch, many are sent English homework that parents should do with them. The child is separated and drilled in the hope of helping him with the language.

In many countries, the policy is to use speaking, listening, and writing as a standard base for communication. Teachers instruct and consider all of these in all lessons The Performance standards in all countries measure how the student can understand the lesson and in England, there are guidelines for learning English as a second language. (ref). E2L in the UK is similar in that communication is not one skill but includes spoken, written and listening among the areas of education. However, in comparison, many countries that have not got a monoglossic approach to teaching in different languages and children learn Arabic, French and English easily alongside each other.

The quality of early years education is when there are aspects of culture in every session so practitioners should know as much as possible about the different cultures. In "Carriers of Hope "it is understood that you cannot teach the English language without understanding a child's own culture and we are using the parents to provide this education for staff. The connections between English and Arabic are supplied by the parent being present to play and add to the knowledge of the group. Play is designed to be informal to allow time for talk.

Comparing and contrasting languages leads to a better understanding of the child's own culture and the host country's culture. The staff ask the parents what's the word for ..so share and celebrate languages. The play with food often leads to sharing what the family eats and how they cook. Many parents bring dishes on festivals,into the group to share, and the circle time songs are presented by parents from different countries.

When the children play dressing up for example "getting married" we talk about how it is in their country of origin. When people get married how many people do they invite? In the comparison, we hear some families will invite hundreds of relatives whilst in UK only a few close family and friends are invited. The honeymoon is often where the most money is spent in the UK, giving the couple a holiday. Whereas in Morocco the money is spent on the wedding for the guests and less attention is on the honeymoon.

In a "Let's Play" We laugh over childbirth differences and schooling differences and chat about family, wives, husbands and money. This gives the English learners a lot to chat about in the group. The quality is in time to try out language, discussions and making mistakes. The children have toys so there are plenty of things to learn the names of in context and by using them.

This stresses the extension from language learning to outside experiences and is very learner-centred and the practitioner is not the only one teaching, women teach other women and translate for them. Ramadam provided an opportunity for real stories from the children that know how it is in their house.

The staff are learning how to not assume how families work. Some of our families live together with extended families bound forever yet in the UK children are expected to leave home and there are often fewer extended families around for the child. These subtleties need to be acknowledged and often grandma comes for a play with the mother and often picks up some English. By comparing different countries the mothers gain a good understanding of their own culture, many of the children need to build pride in their beginnings when society holds up English as the best way to speak this can be hard.

It was clear to see the delight on a mother's face in a refuge when the slides and discussion were about Vietnam. This lady went on to learn great English at a pace before she left the refuge.

Assessment

A major principle of teaching anything is a formative and summative assessment. Black et al (2004) used results from a UK classroom to inform practice. They found there must be a change of roles and skills in the classroom to get the process right for all to learn at their own pace. Good teaching and learning are focused on the process rather than the summative assessment at the end of a test. The method used in "Let's Play" is a performance-based assessment where practitioners can see each child and each mother as an individual and realise not all have English nor the means to learn it at home.

This brings us to another interesting point about teaching English as a foreign language (EFL). Each school of thought about how language is learnt will bring its own methods and approaches. In some classes, no translation is allowed so only the target language is used. It is true that some nurseries only provide English stories and songs even when they have one French child or one Polish child.

The "Let's Play" is lucky to have 13 different languages sometimes and all the children play together. The practitioner is not so locked into teaching English but looks at the relationship between the practitioner and the learners, the dialogue is provided with context and if individuals ask -there is an example to rule given. Usually, other women correct the English used in the group and they chat about why and how the verb has changed.

This is the sort of theory that early years workers may benefit from to back up their style of managing minority language speakers. Communicative language teaching (CLT) is a very lingual method that practices dialogues and learners' errors are a part of the learning. This means the speaker is not corrected over and over or made to say it until it is right. It is just accepted until they correct themselves when hearing others speak. The opposite ALM method relies on the teacher ensuring there are no errors by correcting them every time they come up. They control the learners by using a central technique which is not contextualised. Dialogues are memorised and this is alien to practitioners when teaching the children language so should not be used on children learning English. They might join in with the refrain but we need to explain what is being said as well!

In conclusion, English language learning through play utilises all the early years practitioners' skills of working with parents relying on their funds of knowledge and developing language through play.

IN THEIR OWN WORDS

12 A SYSTEMATIC REVIEW OF THE LITERATURE (SECONDARY RESEARCH)

To create a good systematic review concerning the inclusion, equality, and participation of refugee and asylum-seeking women in higher education, you can follow the steps below:

Develop a clear research question: A good research question is essential for a systematic review. It helps define the review's scope and provides a clear direction. For instance, "What are the barriers to the inclusion, equality, and participation of refugee and asylum-seeking women in higher education?"

Next, define your inclusion and exclusion criteria: This step is crucial in ensuring that your systematic review is comprehensive and relevant. You need to decide on the specific characteristics of the studies you will include, such as the type of participants, type of interventions, and outcome measures.

Then this needs lots of focus so carry it out fresh and conduct a comprehensive literature search: A thorough search for relevant literature is vital to ensure that your review is comprehensive and relevant. Use academic databases such as Google Scholar, Web of Science, and PubMed, as well as other sources such as organisational websites, reports, and government publications. If you do not know how to use a tool ask in the library or get a private tutor. This is one of those things that are rarely taught so students avoid it and use Google Scholar or someone else's references.

The next part is tedious but so worth doing. Screen and select studies: Screening and selecting studies that meet your inclusion criteria is a critical step in the review process. It involves reading the title, abstract, and full text of each study to determine its relevance and eligibility. This cuts down your reading because you don't read all of the papers.

Now the exciting bit is to extract data and assess the quality of the studies: Extracting data from the selected studies and assessing the quality of the studies is essential in ensuring the validity of the findings. You can use a data extraction form to record relevant data, such as study design, sample size, intervention, and outcome measures.

If the last step is done well this step is easy. Synthesising the findings involves summarising and analysing the results of the included studies. You can use a narrative or meta-analysis approach to present the findings, depending on the nature and number of the studies.

In order to interpret and report the findings you may need another analytical brain to bounce ideas off. The final step is to interpret and report the findings. You should provide a comprehensive summary of the findings, including any limitations and implications for future research.

In conclusion, a good systematic review requires careful planning, a comprehensive literature search, and a thorough analysis of the included studies. By following the steps above, you can create a systematic review that provides valuable insights into the inclusion, equality, and participation of refugee and asylum-seeking women in higher education. The supervisor or private tutor will be able to guide you when you get to a difficult step. The following headings can be used to write up your review -This is called secondary research since you did not have people whom you researched with.

A systematic review concerning the inclusion, equality and participation of refugee and asylum-seeking women in Higher Education.

Background

A global refugee crisis has resulted in many UK areas receiving refugees and asylum seekers who are forcibly displaced into new cultures. Educational opportunities aid the process of acculturation. Research has focused on how host countries should increase awareness and access to mental health and maternity services. Still, this review aims to discuss the gap in educational access for adult women refugees and asylum seekers. Factors related to education can help or hinder acculturation. This systematic literature review seeks to put forward evidence that there is a link between educational relevant outcomes and early intervention for refugees that have not yet have the right to remain. The reviewer has a PhD in innovative and inclusive education from Warwick University UK and has developed informal education programmes with refugees in a charity called Carriers of Hope (Coventry UK.). The experience of teaching English and childcare and education modules has led to my research about refugee women in challenging situations.

Search Strategy

Boolean search was done on Google Scholar, Jistor, World of Science and Ebesco. The exact phrase was "Refugee And Higher Education OR tertiary education.

Google Scholar was also used to ensure I had the full literature about refugee and university education. Later a full search was made in the collection to identify if anyone had researched with women; specifically, they had yet to.

Explicit Statement of the Review Questions

This review aimed to systematically examine research to promote education for refugee and asylum-seeking women. Of special interest are the barriers to inclusion and praxis in the UK.

Methodology

This systematic review was performed in accordance with the preferred reporting items for systematic reviews and meta-analysis (PRISMA). Moher et al. 2009 Google Scholar is used to check systematic reviews. The search was carried out from Dec 2021 to March 2022. Three databases were used, and some references were found in the literature cited by the found papers.

Web of Science 192 references that picked up asylum seekers and women and reported on Maternity services and parenthood. Using one reference that explored the education experience, new words were found.

Four databases were searched; PsycINFO, ERIC (Education Resources Information Centre), the British Educational Index and the Australian Educational Index. The search terms employed were: refugee AND (university OR higher education OR tertiary education). Also, I snowballed the information given as references to ensure all relevant articles were included and added a reference management system to Mendeley.

Inclusion and Exclusion Criteria

All of the retrieved studies were assessed against the inclusion and exclusion criteria outlined in Table 1. Inclusion and exclusion criteria for the review and how the studies were grouped for synthesis

Inclusion	Exclusion
Refugee	No reports on identity
Adults experiences	No children or young people
English language	No reviews
Empirical research with refugees and tutors	No commentaries, discussions or grey material

Concerned university access Concerned tertiary education	No books
Equality issues barriers and obstacles	Took out studies in camps /schools
	Took out mental health/maternity
	Refugees from Hitlers time accounts
	Book reviews
	Not children of refugees or second generation

It is common practice for academic databases such as Science Direct, Elsevier, Sage, Bera, Wiley Inter Science, and ProQuest to include only studies published in peer-reviewed journals. This is because the peer-review process involves the evaluation of the research methodology, data analysis, and interpretation by other experts in the field, which helps to ensure the quality and reliability of the research findings.

However, it is essential to note that peer-reviewed journals may not always guarantee the absence of bias or methodological flaws in the research. Furthermore, limiting searches to papers published in English may exclude valuable research conducted in other languages.

Excluding grey literature, such as unpublished research, reports, and conference proceedings, can also limit the scope of research findings. On the other hand, grey literature may contain valuable information and perspectives unavailable in peer-reviewed journals.

Therefore, while using peer-reviewed journals as a source of research is a good practice, it is also important to consider other sources of information, such as grey literature and studies published in different languages, to gain a comprehensive understanding of a particular topic.

What is Grey Literature?

Grey literature refers to research not published in traditional commercial or academic channels, such as peer-reviewed journals or books. This can include conference proceedings, technical reports, working papers, dissertations, government documents, and other types of unpublished research.

The term "grey literature" was first used in the mid-1970s by the British Library's Scientific Information Service, recognising the importance of non-commercial research in science, technology, and medicine. The term "grey" was used to describe this type of literature because it was considered "in-between" the published and unpublished and not easily accessible or searchable through traditional bibliographic databases.

Grey literature can be a valuable source of information for researchers, particularly in areas where the research is rapidly evolving or where traditional publishing channels may need to be more available or appropriate. However, because grey literature is often not subject to the same quality control processes as conventional publishing, it is vital to critically evaluate the sources and methods used in the research before relying on the findings.

Further Limitations and Exclusions

A comprehensive literature search of peer-reviewed articles in three databases The range of papers chosen for the search is ten years; this is not a random choice but matches asylum seekers' legislation for education. There has been a conservative government in the UK over the last ten years. During that time, there has been legislation for asylum seekers' education and .... bills for refugee women working in the UK

Eliminating Words for the Search Terms

Search 1 was very general, consisting of education +asylum seekers +refugees +women.

The term women never came into the search papers and in the full-text reading stage, it was difficult to ascertain if the sample group were men or women because they reported on student numbers, not gender.

Searches took on a variety of keywords and grew more refined • refugee. Some words threw the search too wide, so had to be removed again:
- refugee students • asylum-seeker(s) • migrants• higher education • university
- equity. Praxis • participation• access• aspirations• transition.

Another search included the terms: Words: acculturation, education, higher education, refugees, and reviews. 28,000 with acculturation as the main subject. So, acculturation was removed as a search term.

The collection had to be honed and cut down, but also needed to include longitudinal trends. The inclusion represented any that attended to the problem of education and refugee women. The peer-reviewed publications about camps education were excluded, and only refugees in host countries. When writing about refugees and higher education Zeus (2011). notes higher education is more accessible in resettlement countries than in refugee situations in camps . "protracted refugee situations," as the UNHCR labels them, a person living in camps or urban settings with little or no civic rights, which means they have no access to education (UNCHR figures at a glance).

Full-text stage from those titles saved in Mendeley led to 30 papers to review after all were excluded and filed on the reference manager.

Prisma

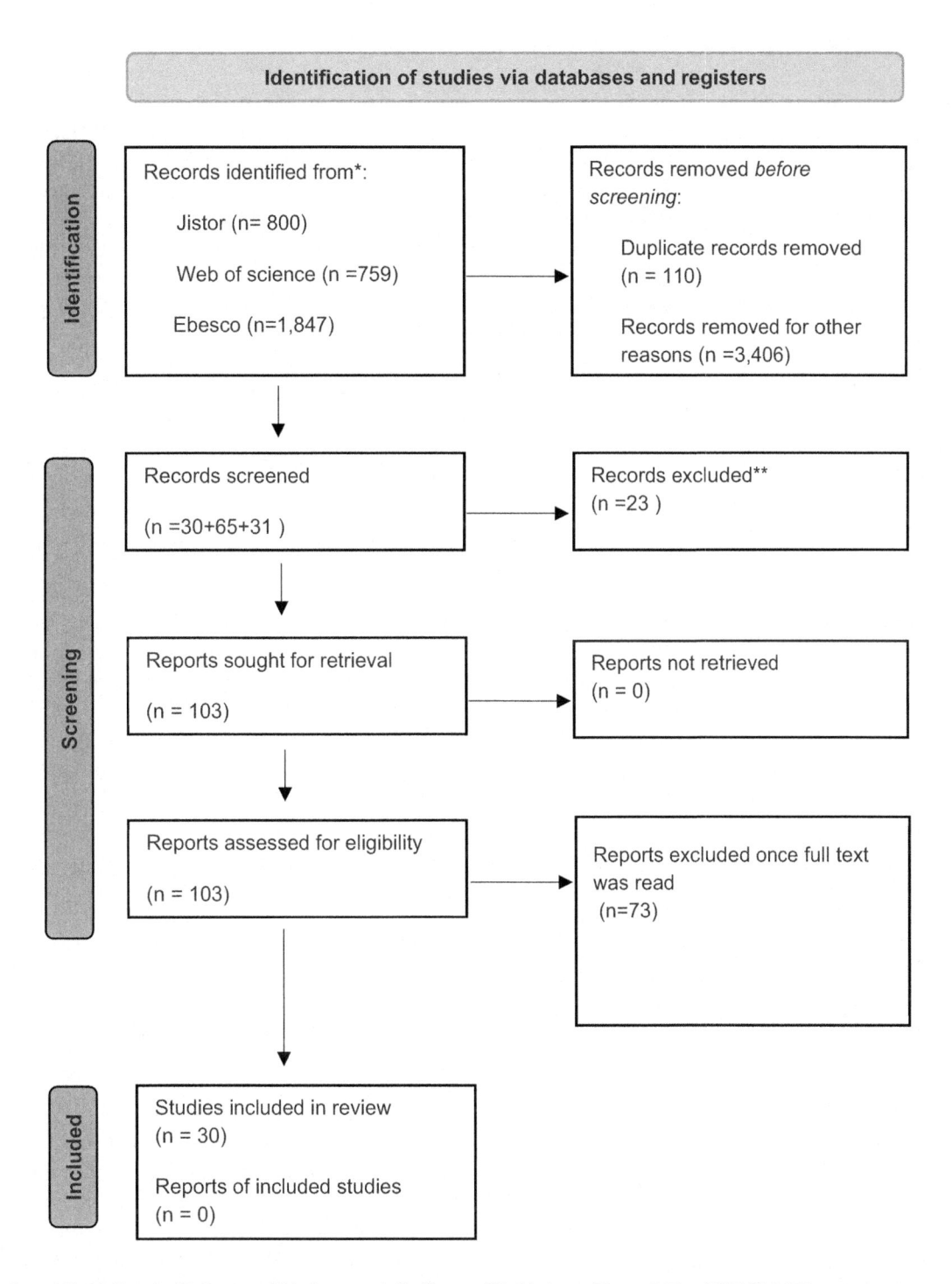

Identification of studies via databases and registers

Identification

Records identified from*:
- Jistor (n= 800)
- Web of science (n =759)
- Ebesco (n=1,847)

Records removed *before screening*:
- Duplicate records removed (n = 110)
- Records removed for other reasons (n =3,406)

Screening

Records screened (n =30+65+31)

Records excluded** (n =23)

Reports sought for retrieval (n = 103)

Reports not retrieved (n = 0)

Reports assessed for eligibility (n = 103)

Reports excluded once full text was read (n=73)

Included

Studies included in review (n = 30)

Reports of included studies (n = 0)

From: Page MJ, McKenzie JE, Bossuyt PM, Boutron I, Hoffmann TC, Mulrow CD, et al. The PRISMA 2020 statement: an updated guideline for reporting systematic reviews. BMJ 2021;372:n71. doi: 10.1136/bmj.n71. For more information, visit: http://www.prisma-statement.org/

The literature catalogue was completed on an Excel sheet. Key themes that helped to interpret the data were the author's discipline, the country they were from, the main points, and how many times they were cited, and this tells the reader who is speaking about what in terms of women refugees and education.

Findings

This review focuses on refugee students' barriers to accessing and enjoying higher education (HE) courses in their host countries. Several key themes emerged from the thematic analysis, including mismatches in expectations between institutions and students, cultural disconnections, the importance of knowing the ropes and feeling a sense of belonging, and limited access to education for adult refugees. The review emphasises the need for interventions that promote social and civic inclusion through education for adults. It highlights how refugees and asylum seekers face exclusion due to a lack of access to technology, basic writing materials, and childcare. The literature also indicates a limited scope in examining the case of refugees in adult education. It is also limited in spread, with most papers coming from Turkey and the USA.

Investing in education has immense benefits, addressing social problems and providing opportunities for self-development, improved finances, and social integration. People from refugee backgrounds often need help to adapt to new cultures, customs, languages, and systems. Barriers to including refugee women in education are prevalent in various areas, such as lack of access to public funds, unfamiliarity with the education application process, and limited awareness of available opportunities. Additionally, refugee women may lack family support for childcare, and government policies often push them into care work. The lack of educational opportunities and exploitation mainly affects women with basic education who aspire to further their education or language skills in a new country.

The inclusion of immigrants and ethnic minorities in the majority society has always been a complex issue, and policies can play a significant role in supporting their inclusion and fostering social cohesion. Aspirations among refugees for qualitative interviews and the need for additional attention from higher education staff to address digital needs among refugee women were also identified. Challenges in higher education for refugees include technological barriers to accessing support and the need for tailored support for their specific needs. National policies often need to address refugees' specific issues, inhibiting opportunities and increasing vulnerability. Austerity cuts and the redirection of funding from educational services for refugees further compound their difficulties in accessing education and integrating into society.

Barriers to HE access include:
Needing more support from employment agencies.
Need for more funding.
Lacking targeted educational funding for refugees.

Challenges in studying a new language and access, participation, and engagement issues were also identified. The psychosocial support needs of refugee students were found to be positively impacted by participating in HE courses. The importance of recognising the learner's identity and context and understanding the context of HE and employment in the host country was emphasised. Education is fundamental to effective integration, leading to better employment prospects and health outcomes.

In conclusion, this research identifies specific barriers to successful educational transition for refugee students, such as language proficiency, differences in teaching approaches and support strategies, mixed messages, lack of support and guidance, inflexibility in educational systems, and external challenges related to finances and accommodation. While the roles of schools and institutions in integrating refugees and asylum-seeking individuals are mentioned, the literature fails to address the education of those without the right to remain, no access to public funds, and no right to education. This exclusionary aspect raises concerns about the "education for all" and WHO educational goals, as education is inaccessible to a significant portion of the refugee population. The research highlights the importance of education for mental health and well-being, making this exclusion even more tragic.

13 WRITE A RATIONALE FOR RESEARCH

Many students rely on political policies or legislation to underpin their arguments, often providing a historical context or using specific terms to frame their work. Tutors in various subjects stay abreast of current news, and it is important for students to also observe and engage with societal issues and their influencers.

In a PhD chapter, one is usually given the rationale of what, who, and why now? Why me? Even smaller studies must set the context before presenting the paper; it is often described as "the wide funnel." that leads to the specific research data.

Research papers are required to have a rationale or justification for several important reasons. The first is to establish the significance of your research. The rationale explains why the research is essential. It establishes the significance of the study by identifying the gap in current knowledge or understanding that the research aims to address. This helps to convince readers, such as researchers and scholars, that the study has a valid purpose and is not redundant or trivial.

The rationale provides context for the research by situating it within the existing body of knowledge. It helps the reader understand how the study fits into the broader field or discipline and how it builds upon or contributes to previous research. This demonstrates that the research is relevant and contributes to advancing knowledge in the field. The rationale helps define the research objectives or questions. It outlines the specific goals or purposes of the study, which guide the research process and shape the methodology and data collection strategies. Clearly defining the objectives allows readers to understand what the research intends to achieve and how it will be conducted.

The rationale justifies the research methodology or approach. It explains why a particular methodology is appropriate for addressing the research objectives and how it will help to gather the necessary data or evidence. This helps to establish the credibility and validity of the research methods used.

Most universities ask for a short rationale before you begin your research to ensure your plan is doable, ethical, and on track. In many cases, research papers must undergo an ethical review process before being conducted. The rationale provides a basis for evaluating the ethical implications of the research, including issues such as potential risks, benefits, and the informed consent process. It helps to demonstrate that the study is ethically sound and justified.

In summary, the rationale in research papers is essential for establishing the significance of the study, providing context, defining objectives, justifying the methodology, and ensuring ethical considerations. It helps convince readers that the research is valuable, relevant, and well-founded and provides a framework for conducting and evaluating the study.

Rationale One

Title: Challenging the Hostile Environment: Efforts to Support Refugees and Migrants in the UK

The term "Hostile Environment" refers to policies that create hardships for refugees and migrants in the UK, particularly those from racialised communities and individuals with insecure immigration status. Coined by the then-Home Secretary, Theresa May, in 2012, the term has become synonymous with these restrictive policies.

In the present climate, where the right to seek asylum in the UK faces challenges and immigration remains a dominant topic in political discourse and media coverage, this research sheds hope. It showcases the tireless efforts of individuals and organisations throughout the United Kingdom who volunteer, campaign and mobilise within NGOs and movements to support those affected by the complex and hostile refugee and migration system. These endeavours demonstrate a genuine concern for preserving Britain's hospitality and fairness values.

Despite the ongoing challenges and debates surrounding immigration, there is a growing public recognition of the importance of supporting refugees and migrants. This research reflects a collective commitment to overcoming barriers and advocating for the inclusion of refugee students in higher education. It highlights the ongoing work of individuals and organisations dedicated to creating a more inclusive and welcoming environment for refugees and asylum seekers in the UK.

Above all, this research serves as a reminder that even in the face of politically driven narratives and media influences, some individuals and groups steadfastly uphold principles of compassion, fairness, and solidarity. Their unwavering dedication to supporting those affected by the refugee and migration system exemplifies the resilience and empathy of communities across the United Kingdom.

Rationale Two

Title: Refugees' Right to Work in the UK: Implications and Challenges in the Post-War and Post-Covid Era

After the Ukraine/Russian war and the COVID-19 pandemic in 2021, a significant moment in UK history emerged: refugees were granted the right to work despite not having the right to remain. Britain's growing demand for care workers has created a unique situation where refugees have been issued work cards without legal residency. This development has prompted discussions on the perception of refugees as a source of cheap labour and concerns about their vulnerability to exploitation due to limited rights and precarious situations.

Brexit and the COVID-19 pandemic have intensified the need for specific personnel in the UK, particularly in the care and hospital sectors. However, it is essential to acknowledge that scholars and organisations focused on refugee and labour rights have raised concerns about the potential exploitation of refugees in the workforce.

Key areas, such as English language acquisition and critical skills relevant to the catering industry, play a vital role in bridging the skills gap. Advisors in education will be responsible for matching individuals' abilities with opportunities and addressing the educational needs of women. This literature review explores whether adult education institutions are adequately prepared for this unique historical stage, considering the policy change allowing refugees to work to address skills gaps.

There is a need for evidence-based research on refugees and education that leads to employment which may be lacking. Recommendations by scholars and experts in the field will provide valuable insights for policymakers and educational service providers in universities and colleges to plan future policies and services.

This review also highlights the barriers women face when entering the education system of host countries, shedding light on the challenges they encounter and the potential solutions that must be addressed.

Rationale Three

Title: Addressing the Impacts of the COVID-19 Pandemic on Vulnerable Refugee and Migrant Communities: Challenges, Responses, and Future Directions

The COVID-19 pandemic, which emerged in March 2020, had far-reaching consequences on a global scale. In the United Kingdom, a series of national lockdowns and various social restrictions disrupted daily life to an unprecedented extent, exposing the country's struggles in managing the pandemic. Among the affected populations, refugee and migrant communities faced unique challenges and were significantly impacted by the pandemic in several ways.

Health and Hygiene: Refugee and migrant communities often struggle to access adequate healthcare and hygiene resources, rendering them more vulnerable to the virus. The presence of overcrowded living conditions in refugee camps and limited access to clean water and sanitation facilities exacerbated the risks.

Disruption of Services: COVID-19 restrictions disrupted essential services provided to refugees, such as education, healthcare, and legal support. Many organisations and NGOs supporting refugees had to adapt their operations, resulting in reduced access to critical services for these communities.

Social Isolation and Mental Health: The pandemic worsened social isolation among refugee and migrant communities. Limited social interaction, separation from loved ones, and the psychological impacts of displacement amplified mental health challenges, including anxiety, depression, and post-traumatic stress disorder.

While the pandemic's peak has subsided in 2023, its enduring social and economic impacts continue disproportionately affecting individuals facing structural disadvantages related to race, gender, economic status, and disability. NGOs at the forefront of support provision had to reshape their structures and services to address new and urgent community needs. Traditional face-to-face activities, such as drop-ins, advice sessions, and public events, were largely suspended.

In response to these challenges, humanitarian organisations, governments, and local communities collaborated to support refugee and migrant communities during the pandemic. Their efforts encompassed distributing hygiene kits, ensuring access to healthcare, facilitating remote education, and providing mental health services. However, sustained support and targeted interventions are crucial to address these communities' specific needs and vulnerabilities during and after the pandemic.

By exploring the challenges faced by refugee and migrant communities during the COVID-19 pandemic, examining the responses implemented by various stakeholders, and identifying future directions for support and intervention, this research aims to shed light on the multifaceted impact of the pandemic and guide the development of effective strategies to mitigate the challenges faced by these vulnerable populations.

Stevens, A.J., Ray, A.M., Thirunavukarasu, A., Johnson, E., Jones, L., Miller, A. and Elston, J.W., 2021. The experiences of socially vulnerable groups in England during the COVID-19 pandemic: a rapid health needs assessment. Public Health in Practice, 2, p.100192.

Dubey, S., Biswas, P., Ghosh, R., Chatterjee, S., Dubey, M.J., Chatterjee, S., Lahiri, D. and Lavie, C.J., 2020. Psychosocial impact of COVID-19. Diabetes & Metabolic Syndrome: clinical research & reviews, 14(5), pp.779-788.

Maldonado, B.M.N., Collins, J., Blundell, H.J. and Singh, L., 2020. Engaging the vulnerable: a rapid review of public health communication aimed at migrants during the COVID-19 pandemic in Europe. Journal of migration and health, 1, p.100004.

Xafis, V., 2020. 'What is Inconvenient for You is Life-saving for Me': How Health Inequities are playing out during the COVID-19 Pandemic. Asian Bioethics Review, 12 Access to Information: Language barriers and limited access to reliable information created challenges for refugees and migrants to stay informed about COVID-19 prevention measures, vaccination campaigns, and other critical updates. (2), pp.223-234.

Rationale Four

Title: Impact of National Politics and Government Support on Poverty, Inequality, and Refugee Issues in the UK

This research inquiry is about the government's support and its implications in the context of ongoing national austerity policies that have exacerbated poverty and inequality in the UK. The country has experienced a series of cuts to public services, including legal aid, and a deepening housing crisis. Additionally, rising interest rates, energy costs, and food bills threaten livelihoods and the financial stability of charities and third-sector support organisations.

Since 2020, there have been multiple changes in the UK Home Secretaries and Ministers of State for Immigration. In September 2021, the Secretary of State for Refugees position was created, but it was removed after two individuals held the post. Throughout this period, national politics in the UK have been marked by volatility and turbulence, with the Conservative party retaining power but witnessing significant political upheaval. Over the past three years, the country has seen three prime ministers and numerous ministerial resignations, sackings, and reshuffles, particularly in key roles related to migration and refugee issues.

This research examines the impact of national politics and government support on poverty, inequality, and refugee-related matters in the UK. By analysing the changing political landscape and its effects on public services, housing, and financial security, this study sheds light on the complex interplay between government policies, political dynamics, and the lived experiences of individuals and communities affected by these issues.

https://www.gov.uk/government/speeches/home-secretary-statement-on-the-illegal-immigration-bill

https://www.theguardian.com/society/2020/mar/03/lost-decade-hidden-story-how-austerity-broke-britain

Rationale Five

Title: The Impact of UK Immigration and Asylum Policy Reforms on Refugee Protection: An Analysis of Recent Legislation

Amid a turbulent political landscape, the United Kingdom's immigration and asylum policy environment has become increasingly challenging. Throughout 2023, the government has implemented far-reaching reforms that pose a significant threat to the country's refugee protection system while perpetuating punitive approaches towards various individuals migrating to the UK. Recent policymaking in refugee and migration issues has been reactive and disjointed, lacking a clear evidence base or consistent rationale. This chaotic atmosphere within the national government has been mirrored in immigration policy, with successive Home Secretaries, Priti Patel and Suella Braverman, championing divisive positions on migration management that have often breached the UK's international human rights obligations and undermined the rule of law.

At the heart of the government's approach lie two pivotal pieces of immigration legislation—the Nationality and Borders Act 2022 and the Illegal Migration Bill. These laws collectively seek to prohibit individuals from seeking asylum in the UK if they enter the country irregularly, irrespective of the merits of their claims. The United Nations High Commissioner on Refugees has characterised this legislation as an "asylum ban," flagging its violation of international law. Moreover, the legislation places the responsibility on the Home Secretary to deport anyone who has entered the UK illegally to either their home country or a safe third country. However, as of now, the UK has only agreed with Rwanda as a potential safe third country, and the legality of this agreement is being contested in court.(June 2023)

The Illegal Migration Bill was introduced to the House of Commons in March 2023 and is currently going through Parliament. In the meantime, an appeal has been filed against the High Court ruling that the Home

Office's fast-track Rwanda removals process is lawful. Asylum Aid and other organisations, including the UNHCR and the UN Special Rapporteur on Trafficking and Freedom from Torture, have supported this appeal. The Court of Appeal heard the case in April 2023, and we are currently awaiting the judgment.

Given the volatile nature of the UK's immigration and asylum policy environment, it is imperative to critically examine the impact of these recent legislative reforms on the country's refugee protection system. This research paper analyses the implications, challenges, and potential consequences of the Nationality and Borders Act 2022 and the Illegal Migration Bill, shedding light on the government's approach and compliance with international legal obligations. By examining the ongoing legal proceedings and considering the broader context, this study seeks to provide a comprehensive understanding of the current state of affairs and stimulate informed discussions on the future of UK immigration and asylum policies. See Diane Taylor, Judges urged to block Home Office plans to send refugees to Rwanda, 27 April 2023, The Guardian. www.theguardian.com/uk-news/2023/ apr/27/judges-urged-to-block-home-office-plans- to-send-refugees-to-Rwanda

Home Office "has no idea."of the impact of immigration policies, Houseof Commons Public Accounts Committee,UK Parliament news article, 18 September 2020. Available at: https://committees.parliament.uk/committee/127/public-accounts-committee/ news/119248/home-office-has-no-idea-of-the- impact-of-immigration-policies/

United Nations High Commissioner on Refugees, Statement on UK Asylum Bill,7 March 2022. Available online at https://www. unhcr.org/uk/news/statement-uk-asylum-bill

UN High Commissioner on Refugees, UNHCR Legal Observations on the Illegal Migration Bill, 2 May 2023 (Updated). www.unhcr.org/uk/sites/uk/files/legacy- pdf/641d7b664.pdf

Rationale Six

Title: The Implications of the Illegal Migration Bill on Human Rights, Asylum Seekers, and Survivors of Trafficking in the UK

Exceptional circumstances have marked the progress of the Illegal Migration Bill through the UK Parliament. Notably, the government needed to have certified the legislation's compatibility with its obligations under the European Convention on Human Rights. Additionally, the allocated time for scrutinising the bill has been significantly reduced. Prime Minister Rishi Sunak has even expressed a willingness to override the House of Lords, if necessary, to ensure the bill's passage. The government has justified its punitive and controversial approach in response to the increasing number of individuals crossing the English Channel in small boats to seek asylum. Although the number of asylum seekers reaching the UK reached a twenty-year high in early 2023, they constitute a small proportion of overall UK immigration. Nonetheless, reducing the number of small boat crossings from France has become central to the Conservative Party's re-election strategy in 2024/25.

The absence of third-country agreements means that many individuals with "inadmissible" asylum claims will likely remain in the UK in limbo for extended periods. According to the Refugee Council, more than 190,000 people could be forced into poverty or detained in the UK over three years due to the Illegal Migration Bill. Shockingly, this includes up to 45,000 children. Moreover, survivors of trafficking will also be fundamentally affected by the bill, as they will be penalised for illegal entry, despite commonly being trafficked into the UK through such means. Approximately two-thirds of current trafficking victims in the UK are estimated to be disqualified from receiving advice, support, reflection and recovery periods, material assistance, a decision on their claim, or protection from removal under the bill. Even those who are not disqualified will face increased difficulties in accessing support and protection.

Chaotic reforms to in-country asylum management have also taken place. In 2022, the government announced a shift to a "full dispersal" policy for individuals seeking asylum in the UK, resulting in approximately 50,000 asylum seekers being housed in refugees and hotels nationwide. Many of these locations need more appropriate support services or networks, posing significant challenges. This arrangement comes at an estimated cost of £6 million per day.

Given the implications of the Illegal Migration Bill, it is crucial to examine the impact on human rights, asylum seekers, and survivors of trafficking in the UK. This research paper aims to analyse the bill's consequences, including its effects on the legal framework for trafficking survivors, the potential increase in poverty and detention, and the shortcomings of the in-country asylum management system. By providing an in-depth evaluation, this study seeks to raise awareness and foster informed discussions on the human rights implications of the bill and its long-term effects on vulnerable populations.

Refugee Council, Illegal Migration Bill - Assessment of the impact of inadmissibility, removals, detention, accommodation and safe routes, March 2023. https://www.refugeecouncil.org.uk/wp-content/uploads/2023/03/Refugee-Council- Asylum-Bill-impact-assessement.pdf

The Independent, Rishi Sunak hints he could overrule Lords on small boats bill, 6 June 2023, https://www.independent.co.uk/ news/UK/politics/sunak-small-boats-asylum- seekers-b2352193.html

House of Commons Library, Asylum statistics, UK Parliament, 1 March 2023. https://commonslibrary.parliament.UK/research- briefings/sn01403/

Home Office, Asylum seekers in receipt of support, by support type, as at December 2010 to as at March 2023, published in National Statistics: How many people do we grant protection to? 25 May 2023. https://www.gov. uk/government/statistics/immigration-system- statistics-year-ending-march-2023/how-many- people-do-we-grant-protection-to

Thousands of asylum seekers to be moved out of hotels, UK Government news story, 5 June 2023. https://www.gov.uk/government/news/ thousands-of-asylum-seekers-to-be-moved- out-of-hotels

Rationale Seven

Title: Comparative Analysis of Government Approaches to Refugee Resettlement and Visa Schemes: A Case Study of Hong Kong and Ukraine

Over the past few years, the United Kingdom has faced significant refugee influxes from different parts of the world. In response to the ongoing crisis in Hong Kong and the war in Ukraine, the UK government implemented bespoke visa schemes to accommodate and support individuals fleeing these regions. This research paper aims to compare the government's approach to refugee resettlement and visa schemes, explicitly focusing on the cases of Hong Kong and Ukraine.

Since 2020, many individuals have sought refuge in the UK from Hong Kong, as China's legislation severely restricted the rights and freedoms of the people there. In response, the UK government introduced the Welcome Programme for Hong Kong British Nationals Overseas (BNOs) in January 2021. As a result, more than 160,000 individuals have applied for UK visas under this program.

Similarly, the conflict in Ukraine, triggered by Russia's invasion in February 2022, prompted the UK government, along with other European countries, to establish bespoke visa pathways for Ukrainian refugees. These schemes have enabled approximately 130,000 people to find refuge in the UK. However, the accommodation provided for these refugees has become controversial, with many individuals residing in hotels without adequate support services or networks, costing an estimated £6 million per day.

The government has proposed relocating refugees to alternative premises such as disused ferries, former prisons, and military bases to address the mounting accommodation costs. Nevertheless, this plan has faced significant opposition from local communities, authorities, and NGOs. Concerns have been raised regarding the potential use of highly securitised, overcrowded, and unsuitable facilities for accommodating large numbers of asylum seekers.

While media coverage of the UK's bespoke visa schemes has generally portrayed them positively, public opinion has primarily expressed sympathy towards recent arrivals from Hong Kong and Ukraine. However, the inconsistent and varying levels of support and security provided by these ad hoc schemes have sparked confusion and controversy. Previous programs for refugees from Syria and Afghanistan have also been subject to criticism, highlighting inconsistencies within the government's approach.

Moreover, the contrasting welcome extended to individuals under these visa schemes compared to the overall hostility of the broader asylum system has led to allegations of discrimination, hypocrisy, and racism within the government's approach. These issues warrant an in-depth examination of the effectiveness, fairness, and coherence of the government's response to the refugee crises in Hong Kong and Ukraine.

By conducting a comparative analysis of the government's approaches to refugee resettlement and visa schemes, this research aims to shed light on the strengths and weaknesses of these initiatives, identify areas for improvement, and contribute to the ongoing discourse on refugee policies and practices in the UK.

UK Government, Press Release, Government announces a third year of support to help Hong Kongers settle into life in theUK, 1 March 2023. https://www.gov.uk/ government/news/government-announces- a-third-year-of-support-to-help-hong-kongers- settle-into-life-in-the-uk

UNHCR, Ukraine-Fastest Growing Refugee Crisis in Europe Since WWII, 6 June 2022. https://www.unhcr.org/hk/en/73141-ukraine- fastest-growing-refugee-crisis-in-europe-since- wwii.html This figure includes Ukrainians who arrived in the UK under both the Ukraine Family Scheme and the Ukraine Sponsorship Scheme. https://www.gov.uk/guidance/ukraine- sponsorship-scheme-visa-data-by-country-upper-and-lower-tier-local-authority

See British Future, Britons welcome Hong Kongers as figures show UK issues over 110,000 BN(O) visas, 26 May 2023. www.britishfuture.org/britons-welcome- hong-kongers-as-figures-show-uk-issues- over-110000-bno-visas/

Collecting Comprehensive Background Evidence for Refugee Research

When researching the topic of refugees coming to the UK, it is essential to maintain a balanced approach that considers multiple perspectives. Regardless of personal opinions or political stances, it is crucial to explore arguments from both sides of the debate and present a comprehensive analysis. Ethical and analytical research requires a fair presentation of facts and opinions, acknowledging the reasoning behind differing viewpoints, even if they contradict personal beliefs.

Collecting background evidence that provides a holistic understanding of the issue is essential to support your research. Consider incorporating a historical section in the appendix, which can be referenced in the main body of your work. Understanding the historical context is crucial, as political changes can significantly impact the landscape surrounding refugee policies and practices. Staying updated with current news related to your research module can also provide valuable insights into the evolving political climate and its implications.

A comprehensive analysis of your reading materials will contribute to higher grades. It is important to consider the implications of your research findings. For instance, the government's policy decisions can directly impact charitable organisations and NGOs. Suppose a charity or NGO has allocated their resources to support families in hotels. In that case, changes in government policy can disrupt their planning and potentially lead to a loss of funding for hotel-related work. Furthermore, if refugee work falls out of favour due to government policies, the many charities dedicated to assisting refugees may need more funds and partnerships. Due to allowing asylum seekers to work in care homes, the charity may change its funding bids to concern itself with employment schemes.

By actively considering the consequences and implications of your research, you can develop a more nuanced and comprehensive understanding of the refugee issue. This approach demonstrates critical thinking and a deeper engagement with the subject matter, ultimately enhancing the quality of your research and analysis.

14 A BOOLEAN SEARCH FOR LITERATURE

George Boole, developed a branch of algebra in the mid-19th century known as Boolean algebra. Boolean algebra is based on the use of logical operators such as "AND," "OR," and "NOT" to manipulate and evaluate logical statements.

In the context of information retrieval, Boolean search refers to a type of search that uses Boolean operators to combine search terms to retrieve more specific and relevant results. The use of Boolean operators in searches was first developed in the early days of computing when databases were first being created. Nowadays, Boolean search is commonly used in search engines, library databases, and other information retrieval systems to help users find the most relevant results for their search queries. (Propositional Logic - Stanford University. http://infolab.stanford.edu/~ullman/focs/ch12.pdf)

To conduct a Boolean search on Google Scholar for COVID and refugee children, use the following operators:

1. AND: Use "AND" to combine search terms and retrieve articles that include both terms. For example, "COVID AND refugee children" will retrieve articles that contain both "COVID" and "refugee children" in their text.
2. OR: Use "OR" to combine search terms and retrieve articles that include either term. For example, "COVID OR pandemic" will retrieve articles that contain either "COVID" or "pandemic" in their text.
3. NOT: Use "NOT" to exclude specific terms from your search. For example, "COVID NOT vaccine" will retrieve articles that contain "COVID" but not "vaccine" in their text.
4. Quotation marks: Use quotation marks to search for an exact phrase. For example, "refugee children" will retrieve articles that contain the exact phrase "refugee children" in their text.
5. Parentheses: Use parentheses to group search terms together. For example, "(COVID OR pandemic) AND (refugee children OR migrant children)" will retrieve articles that contain either "COVID" or "pandemic" and either "refugee children" or "migrant children" in their text.

Here's an example of how to conduct a Boolean search on Google Scholar for COVID and refugee children:

("COVID-19" OR "coronavirus") AND ("refugee children" OR "migrant children")

In this search, parentheses group the terms "COVID-19" and "coronavirus" together because they relate to the same concept. Next, quotation marks search for "refugee children" and "migrant children" to retrieve articles using those terms. Finally, the AND operator retrieves articles containing both "COVID-19" or "coronavirus" and "refugee children" or "migrant children."

Using Boolean search operators, narrow down search results and retrieve relevant articles. Consult your supervisor or private tutor to help narrow down search terms.

Young Refugee Children and the effects of COVID-19 in England

This literature review enabled a paper about Covid. Often students are just given the job to write an essay but need to learn how to start it. This will help!

To get the key concepts or an overview of what literature is in the field already, you can start with Google Scholar. Many tutors tell their students to refrain from using Google Scholar, but it is the quickest way to get a peer-reviewed paper for your writing.

Tutors may caution against relying solely on Google Scholar for several reasons. Firstly, Google Scholar has limited coverage, as it may include only some academic journals and may have gaps in specific fields. This means that certain subscription-based journals or articles behind paywalls may not be accessible, which can limit the completeness of your research.

Secondly, Google Scholar needs more strict quality control measures. Unlike curated databases and academic search engines, it includes many sources, including preprints, conference papers, and non-peer-reviewed content. These sources may not undergo the same rigorous review process as articles published in reputable journals, making assessing their credibility and reliability challenging.

Thirdly, evaluating sources can be difficult on Google Scholar. The search algorithm prioritises highly cited articles, which may only sometimes align with the most relevant or current research for your specific needs. Additionally, Google Scholar may have limited advanced search techniques and filters compared to specialised academic databases, making it harder to refine searches and find the most suitable sources. Lastly, Google Scholar's search functionality is relatively basic compared to specialised academic databases. It may need advanced features commonly found in those databases, such as field-specific search options, citation searching, or the ability to refine search results based on specific criteria. These advanced features can assist researchers in finding more precise and targeted information.

Despite these limitations, Google Scholar can still be a valuable tool for a broader research strategy. It can help you discover relevant articles and serve as a starting point for further exploration. However, tutors often advise students to utilise various research sources, including specialised databases, library catalogues, and subject-specific resources, to ensure a more comprehensive and reliable understanding of the topic.

For this piece, I used a Boolean to search Google Scholar for "Covid AND refugee children." This brought up social support, missing school, Szelei et al. (2022) and lone refugee children in the UK.(Bhatti-Sinclair 2021)

Szelei, N., Devlieger, I., Verelst, A., Spaas, C., Jervelund, S.S., Primdahl, N.L., Skovdal, M., Opaas, M., Durbeej, N., Osman, F. and Soye, E., 2022. migrant students' sense of belonging and the Covid-19 pandemic: Implications for educational inclusion. Social Inclusion, 10(2), pp.172-184.

Bhatti-Sinclair, K., 2021. Unaccompanied asylum-seeking children and young refugees: Alone in the UK in a pandemic. Social Work and COVID-19: Lessons for Education and Practice, 23.

I had to improve my search and examine what I wanted to search for. I needed the government's response to provide a background to my work in Carriers of Hope. I needed to sketch out what I thought was my argument.

Then I listed the top 10 papers on my computer. I was writing in November 2021, so there must be a lot more COVID-19 writings now, but sadly, the refugee children are often missed from research. If you do want to write about refugee children, choose a topic! I worry about plagiarism so I am careful to re write or highlight a copy.

Do a mini-lit review on each topic- use the strip method to get everything out and onto a Word document. Here is an ordered argument highlighting that refugee children were worse off than all other children during COVID-19:

1. The outbreak of COVID-19 in England led to the closure of schools and nurseries for nearly all pupils, affecting children's education and socialisation.
2. Refugee children faced additional challenges during the extended lockdown and school closures, including child poverty, bereavement, and hunger.
3. The UK had the highest number of COVID-19 deaths in Europe, increasing stress and anxiety among families, including refugees.
4. The UK government's slow response and inconsistent advice further exacerbated the challenges of refugee children and their families.
5. Refugee women, unable to work until they had the right to remain, were confined to small spaces with their children, leading to increased food insecurity and limited resources for necessities.
6. The cost of masks was out of reach for many refugee families, and the lack of technology hindered their ability to access online resources for education and support.
7. Refugee children relied on limited access to technology, worked on their mothers' phones, and lacked adequate home-school support, leading to increased stress and challenges in completing assignments.
8. The closure of schools meant refugee children missed out on free school meals and socialisation opportunities while their families struggled to provide enough food at home.
9. Refugee families faced difficulties accessing food banks and other support services due to isolation or COVID-19-related restrictions.
10. The attainment gap between poorer and more affluent children typically widens during summer holidays, and the lockdown exacerbated this gap, particularly affecting the most disadvantaged groups, including refugee children.
11. Refugee children experienced the worst effects of the digital divide, facing challenges in educational attainment and mental health compared to more affluent households.

Then create an outline for each key point- following the steps in this video. Here's a lit review overview (for non-systematic) https://youtu.be/rk_jgtdJOD0

Obviously if you can manage to organise this into two issues say education and technology you could go deeper into a section in your literature. I wanted the coverage of all the additional activities in carriers of Hope so kept it wide.

Silent Suffering: Unveiling the Impact of the Pandemic on Refugee Children in Extended Lockdown and School Closures

In March 2020, the world witnessed an unprecedented disruption in the face of a relentless and unforeseen adversary – the COVID-19 pandemic. As governments scrambled to implement containment measures, one of the critical decisions made by authorities across England was the closure of schools and nurseries, affecting the lives of countless young learners. While this measure was undoubtedly necessary to safeguard public health, it also inadvertently thrust a vulnerable segment of society into a uniquely challenging situation – refugee children. This reflection is centred on examining the impact of the pandemic on these young individuals as they found themselves confined to their homes during extended lockdowns and school closures. Amidst the growing literature on the effects of COVID-19, one concerning gap stands out – the limited focus on child poverty, bereavement, and hunger, particularly in the context of refugee children. Most existing papers primarily concentrate on children and education, leaving a noticeable absence of publications concerning the experiences of asylum-seeking families during the pandemic. This work, therefore, seeks to fill this void by offering a reflective account, shedding light on the hardships endured by refugee children during these trying times. By delving into their unique challenges and unearthing their resilient spirit, this reflection aims to advocate for greater attention and support for this vulnerable group, fostering a more inclusive and compassionate response to future crises.

The U.K. has the highest number of deaths from COVID-19 in Europe. O.N.S. Nov 2021 shows that the death rate is going up in England and Wales. In the week ending 05 November 2021 (Week 44), 11,550 deaths were registered in England and Wales; this was 563 more deaths than the previous week (Week 43) and 16.8% above the five-year average (1,659 more deaths.

International readers must understand the context of the English COVID-19 situation. Although there is a free National Health Service and a structured education system, families are affected by the U.K. having the highest death rate per 100,000 population in the world. This stress is added because the U.K. had ten years of austerity under the Conservative Government and just managed pressure due to the U.K. leaving the European Union. (Brexit 2020). Also, compared to other countries, the Government adapted very slowly to try and stop the virus spread and offered confusing and inconsistent advice, according to Holt and Murray (2021). At first, the Government advised the country to do a minimal intervention, hoping the population would gain "herd immunity ", a notion criticised by Ferguson et al. (2020), who reported that minimal intervention would overwhelm the health systems.

The Government then announced a school and nursery closure and lockdown from 23 March 2020. There followed six months of missed schooling, which affected the debate and publication of literature that school was not just for education but also socialisation and containment. Holt, L. and Murray, L., 2022. Children and COVID-19 in the UK. Children's Geographies, 20(4), pp.487-494.

For the female refugees and asylum seekers in my group, Carriers of Hope, a Coventry charity, the notion that a disease was coming frightened many mothers. They reported that their child was too scared to go out because the germs would kill them. So, before the lockdown, the group activity was changed to learn about COVID-19 and how to keep ourselves safe. However, this group of refugee women needed disinfectants, masks, or hand cleaners and generally struggled to get food daily. The Facebook for Carriers called out to get supplies for our families. Like so many times before, the people of Coventry supported the refugee families and donated what we needed. We were concerned about all the incorrect information being spread by the communities of refugees. So we created a "what's app" to keep the families in touch with us, and this free technology became the educational and healthcare systems for women and their children. This was especially important for children who lived in smaller homes without gardens because the parks were closed, and people were fined if they went out. The women reported that the daily contact with others from their group was appreciated and "kept them sane".

The UK considered children with interventions for abuse and neglect and educational health care plans; children of essential workers could attend their nursery or school. However, refugee women are not allowed to work until they have the right to remain, which left many refugees and asylum-seeking women in a room with all their children during the lockdown. In addition, the women with babies in the Coventry refuge shared a kitchen and living room with 20 other mums and babies so social distancing was impossible and when one got COVID-19 they all got it, including the babies . The hardships of finding food but not being able to go and not having the technology to order food online led to food insecurity worse than the normal situation.

Another problem was that masks were compulsory, but the cost of masks was out of reach for many people. In the refuge, one woman made the other masks from the materials and sewing machine Carriers of Hope supplied. The charity also had a refugee woman who made and sold masks to the public online and asked them to buy another for women in the refugee community. In this way, many could go out for an hour of exercise. In addition, having a mask affected their children's well-being as they could get some respite from the small room that was home.

Richardson and Serllgreen (2020) report that schools struggled to cope with social distancing, especially among younger children. In a complete turnaround from the moral panic about children spending too much time online, they were required to spend hours in front of a computer. Home-schooling online became a strategy, and the Government offered some support and a range of specific resources for home-schooling. Greenway and Eaton-Thomas (2020).

This added to the stress for the refugee women, especially if they had other children of different ages. The reports that the "homework" set for the children went on for hours and hours. The children and their mums only sometimes knew which online resources to push at the children. They had no printer, so they had to work out homework online. Of course, the family's technology skills increased as they learnt how to use apps and programmes and email the school.

The younger children no longer attended "Lets Play" with Carriers of Hope but did activities at home, videoed them and uploaded them to "What's app" so other families could see what was occupying them. The staff ensured stories and songs were uploaded and delivered creative materials to each house, leaving them on the doorstep.

The children who did have a place at school could see their work online and were given pens, pencils and paper from C.O.H. to complete it. At the same time, Department for Education supported the hours and hours of online work despite teachers getting burnt out. The Government also offered guidance on safeguarding and online safety. (Department of Education 2020.)

The impact of lockdown on children's mental health and well-being has been identified by The Children's Society (2020), and the Children's Commissioner for England has emphasised the inequalities that children suffer from lockdown and home-schooling. There are many limitations for the refugees and asylum seekers during COVID-19 because they are often poorer educated families and ethnic minorities in overcrowded situations. There are also families in refugees or temporary accommodation, families fleeing slavery, and sex workers with mental ill-health issues.

Stresses that the closure of schools caused was evident in the refugee group. Children would get free school meals, but now they were at home, and the family needed more food. The women asked for help to get to food banks but could not do this if someone in the family had COVID-19 or was isolated. This can be compared to other children who were being fed but missed socialisation. "Due to school closing, I'm missing out on a huge chunk of education that can prepare me for secondary school and later life. That makes me feel unprepared and not ready for the journey ahead. Despite doing the same subjects, I miss a sense of structure in my life. I miss socialising with my friends and laughing with them." Girl, 11 Children's Commissioner Lockdown Experiences (2020).

C.O.H. then set up world food banks, realising the tinned goods from food banks in Coventry were not suitable for the worldwide refugees and their families. The charity had to adapt quickly to find space to store any fresh food donations and then find a system to get them to people's doorsteps; However, the food bag was only sufficient for three days; it helped the children alongside the donations from other charities.

The gap between the attainment of poorer and more affluent children usually increases over the summer holidays. Stewart, Watson and `Campbell (2018) reported a lack of quality activities, and food poverty is critical to this gap. Social class, racial and ethnic, are affecting the most disadvantaged groups. Longfield, children's commissioner for England (2020), pointed out that lockdown would worsen the usual attainment gap and social mobility. Andrew et al. (2020) wrote that home learning support is more likely to be bought and paid for in more affluent households. The children of refugees got the worst of the digital divide, educational attainment measures, and mental health challenges, explained Bayrakdar, and Guveli (2020).

Conclusion

As we reflect on the impact of the COVID-19 pandemic on refugee children during extended lockdowns and school closures, it becomes evident that this vulnerable group experienced silent suffering amidst the chaos and uncertainty that engulfed the world. The virus outbreak in March 2020 led to the closure of schools and nurseries across England, affecting the lives of countless young learners, including those seeking refuge in the country.

This reflective account highlights the gap in the existing literature, where the focus on child poverty, bereavement, and hunger among refugee children during the pandemic remains limited. While numerous papers concentrate on the impact of COVID-19 on children's education, the experiences of asylum-seeking families have often been overlooked, creating a void in research that must be addressed.

In the context of the U.K., the pandemic's toll on public health and the subsequent lockdown measures compounded the challenges faced by refugee families, especially those living in cramped accommodations and enduring financial hardships. The death rate in the country reached alarming levels, adding stress to an already strained social and economic landscape due to ten years of austerity and the uncertainties surrounding Brexit.

For refugee children and their families, the lockdown presented unique hardships. Restricted from working until they obtained the right to remain, many refugee women found themselves confined to overcrowded living spaces with all their children, leaving little room for social distancing. The closure of schools and nurseries resulted in six months of missed schooling, exacerbating the digital divide and educational challenges. The lack of access to technology hindered their ability to participate in online education, and even those who could engage in remote learning faced increased stress and pressure to juggle multiple age groups and subjects.

Food insecurity loomed large for refugee families during the pandemic, with children missing out on free school meals and limited access to food banks due to isolation or COVID-19 infections within the household. Carriers of Hope, a Coventry charity, stepped in to provide these families with essential food supplies and masks, but the struggle for necessities persisted.

The pandemic further widened the gap in educational attainment and mental health challenges for refugee children, compounding existing inequalities. The lack of quality activities, exacerbated by food poverty and the digital divide, led to a worrying increase in the attainment gap between disadvantaged groups and their more affluent peers.

However ,it is crucial to recognise the resilience and strength of refugee children and their families during these trying times. The world may have largely overlooked their silent suffering, but our understanding of their struggles urges us to advocate for greater attention and support for this vulnerable group. The lessons learned from this research call for a more inclusive and compassionate response from governments, policymakers, and communities, ensuring that the well-being and future of refugee children are not compromised in the face of future crises. Through collective efforts and empathetic understanding, we can pave the way for a more equitable and hopeful tomorrow for all children, regardless of their circumstances. "Silent Suffering" reminds us we must not let their experiences go unheard. Still, instead, we must act to alleviate their burdens and provide a nurturing environment where they can flourish and grow.

15 ACKNOWLEDGING THE RESEARCHER'S LENS - NAVIGATING BIAS IN SCIENTIFIC INQUIRY

This chapter explores the crucial aspect of identifying bias as a researcher and understanding its potential impact on scientific or scholarly research. From personal beliefs and preconceived notions to funding sources and societal backgrounds, we delve into the various factors that can unintentionally influence research outcomes. By shedding light on these biases, we strive to uphold scientific rigour and objectivity, encouraging researchers to adopt methodologies that minimise bias and promote transparency in their reporting. Through self-awareness and critical analysis, researchers can navigate the complexities of bias and contribute to more robust and reliable research findings.

For many students, the first task set out in a PhD is to write about their life and what has influenced this. The work is usually pages and pages of life stories. It could be more useful not as a chapter but to ensure the student is aware of their own bias in the research. When we read papers that quote certain studies and organisations, we decide if the information is good or biased, for example, selling a particular story. We might decide that all of our references are white writers and need to read more from other research sections.

Writing about your bias in the research section can be for several reasons, but minimising bias in scientific or scholarly research is generally considered necessary. Bias refers to a systematic error or deviation from the truth when there is partiality or preference towards a particular perspective, result, or conclusion. Here are a few potential reasons why bias might be present in research reporting: researchers have their own beliefs, values, and perspectives. These personal factors can sometimes unintentionally influence how they interpret data or present their findings. Conscious or unconscious biases can affect the selection of data, the interpretation of results, and the overall tone and emphasis of the report.

Also, researchers might have preconceived concepts or hypotheses about their study topic, which can influence their approach and analysis. These biases can lead to a selective presentation of data that supports their initial beliefs while neglecting contradictory evidence.

I often look at the publishers of a paper for funding and conflicts of interest. Organisations or entities sometimes fund research studies with a vested interest in particular outcomes. This can create conflicts of interest that may introduce bias into the research process. Researchers might feel pressured to produce results that align with the interests of their funders, potentially compromising the objectivity and integrity of the study.

To ensure their work is important many writers will make their results up! Academic and professional environments often reward positive and statistically significant results. Researchers may feel compelled to highlight substantial findings or downplay insignificant or negative results to increase their chances of publication or career advancement. This can introduce bias by selectively reporting data or emphasising certain aspects over others.

To maintain scientific rigour and objectivity, researchers are encouraged to be aware of their biases and take steps to minimise them. This includes using rigorous research methodologies, conducting blind or double-blind experiments, transparently reporting methods and results, acknowledging limitations, and encouraging peer review and replication of studies to ensure the reliability and validity of research findings.

These are my biases to consider as the research is read; I work for a charity, Carriers of Hope; I am a parent of three boys, so I have experience giving birth in the U.K. and have no experience living in a country as a refuge. I am a white Irish female; my family came to Coventry in the 1940s looking for work. I have had an experience of childhood poverty and living in a slum. I struggled with education. I have a diagnosis of severe dyslexia.

16 ETHNOGRAPHY AS A CHOICE OF METHOD - EXPLORING THE DYNAMICS OF RESEARCHING LIVED EXPERIENCES

The method of ethnography is a powerful tool for collecting data and gaining insight into the lived experiences of various groups. Ethnography offers a unique perspective, enabling researchers to immerse themselves in their subjects' social and cultural contexts, leading to a deeper understanding of their world. Researchers must choose a method and all of us have to examine the impact of choosing different data collection techniques, such as interviews and focus groups, and how they can influence the richness and complexity of the obtained data.

What is ethnography? Ethnography goes beyond mere data collection; it involves immersing oneself in the cultural and social settings of the subjects under study.

This is a method of collecting data, one of many because you can choose focus groups or interviews. How would the data change if the researcher carried out focus groups or interviews but were alien to the participant group?

Participant observation has been used in all sorts of research like;

- Alfadhli, K. and Drury, J., 2018. The role of shared social identity in mutual support among refugees of conflict: An ethnographic study of Syrian refugees in Jordan. Journal of Community & Applied Social Psychology, 28(3), pp.142-155.
- Connor Schisler, A.M. and Polatajko, H.J., 2002. The Individual as Mediator of thePerson-Occupation-Environment Interaction: Learning from theExperience of Refugees. Journal of Occupational science, 9(2), pp.82-92.
- Lipson, J.G., Weinstein, H.M., Gladstone, E.A. and Sarnoff, R.H., 2003. Bosnian and Soviet refugees' experiences with health care. Western Journal of Nursing Research, 25(7), pp.854-871.

The Researcher's Profile

The obvious thing to consider is if you have access to the group you would like to research with, do you have a particular profile to get into a position to research? To gain trust in a group of teenagers it may not be best to send in a very old researcher in. a track suit . Opportunities to carry out ethnography should fit the researcher's life. If the student hopes to consider ethnography the ethics of why and how are considered especially if they hope to become an insider.

The concept of insider/outsider is interesting in research methods because it addresses the researcher's positionality to the community or group being studied. It refers to the extent to which the researcher is part of or detached from the social and cultural context of the participants.

When considering bias the situation has to be assessed honestly, you cannot be friends and a researcher without some deep analysis. A researcher who is an insider, meaning they belong to the community being studied, may have a deeper understanding of the culture, language, and norms of the group. While this can be advantageous in building trust and rapport with participants, it may also introduce biases that can influence data collection and interpretation. On the other hand, an outsider researcher might need a different level of understanding but can offer a more objective view of the community.

Recognising one's insider or outsider status encourages researchers to engage in reflexivity. Researchers must critically reflect on how their background, beliefs, and experiences might shape their perceptions and interactions with participants. Awareness of these potential biases can help maintain a more balanced and transparent research process.

If the research is with people you have worked closely with for some time it may be you are trusted by some of the participants and they could be the ones that conduct the research as in citizens research or you might use them to run the focus groups .Being an insider may grant more straightforward access to the community and its members, as they might be more willing to participate in research conducted by someone they see as part of their group. However, it can also raise concerns about objectivity and conflicts of interest. While facing potential challenges in gaining trust initially, an outsider may bring a fresh perspective and be perceived as more impartial.

The researcher's positionality can raise ethical questions, particularly in studies involving vulnerable or marginalised groups. Being an insider might lead to concerns about confidentiality, power dynamics, and potential exploitation. These issues need careful consideration when researching sensitive topics or populations. I consider this when supporting women in the groups to become leaders for any projects.

The insider/outsider status can influence data collection and interpretation. Insiders are more adept at understanding subtle cultural nuances, while outsiders provide a more critical perspective that challenges established assumptions.

The insider/outsider status can shape the researcher-participant relationship. An insider may share a sense of belonging and understanding, creating a more relaxed atmosphere for participants to share their experiences. Alternatively, an outsider may be seen as an unbiased observer, encouraging participants to respond more candidly.

Understanding the researcher's positionality is crucial in determining the validity and generalisability of research findings. Transparency about the researcher's insider or outsider status allows readers to assess the potential impact on the results and consider the applicability of findings to other contexts.

In conclusion, the insider/outsider perspective in research methods is intriguing because it highlights the complex interplay between the researcher and the researched. By acknowledging and addressing positionality, researchers can enhance the quality and rigour of their work and contribute to a more comprehensive understanding of the studied phenomenon. By saying I work with refugee women and children I do not say I am expert I just say I know of some lived experiences.

Going Native

As researchers become more integrated into the community they are studying, they may develop personal attachments and emotional connections with the participants. This emotional involvement can make it challenging to remain impartial when analysing and interpreting the data, potentially leading to biased findings. It might be the write up sounds critical of institutions when the researcher emphasises with their participants .Readers might pick up on the research bias when the writer misses it.

"Going native" can compromise the integrity of the research process, as the researcher may unconsciously favour information that aligns with their adopted perspective. This can lead to selective reporting of data and the neglect of contradictory evidence.

The process of "going native" raises questions about the researcher's identity and the potential blurring of boundaries between the researcher and the researched. Researchers may find themselves grappling with questions about their role, positionality, and how their personal experiences and beliefs intersect with their research. This is why the supervisor must examine issues that impact the research and the researcher's identity.

The phenomenon of "going native" raises ethical concerns, mainly when researchers study vulnerable or marginalised communities. Researchers must be aware of the power dynamics and ensure that their interactions with participants are respectful and do not exploit or harm them. If it is decided that every participant receives some nappies a note must be kept of this.

Researchers need to engage in reflexivity throughout the research process to critically examine their biases and preconceptions. The risk of "going native" underscores the importance of being conscious of these biases and actively working to mitigate their influence on the research. Ethnographic research often involves deep immersion in the community under study to understand their experiences better. However, researchers must balance immersing themselves enough to gain insights while maintaining a critical distance to uphold objectivity. This is particularly important for child protection disclosures, and they should be reported even if it spoils a good research piece.

The potential influence of "going native" on data interpretation raises questions about the validity and reliability of research findings. It highlights the need for researchers to be transparent about their experiences during the research process and how these experiences may have influenced their interpretations.

In conclusion, the concept of "going native" in research methods is a cautionary reminder of the delicate balance between immersion and objectivity in ethnographic research. By being aware of this phenomenon and actively managing their roles as researchers, individuals can ensure the validity and trustworthiness of their findings while respecting the communities they study.

Navigating Ethnography in Institutional Settings: Balancing Objectivity and Ethical Considerations

Ethnographic research presents a unique opportunity to delve into the lived experiences of diverse communities. However, conducting research within institutions, such as schools or hospitals, raises critical considerations. This article explores the complexities of undertaking ethnography in institutional settings, where researchers may encounter challenges addressing detrimental issues and potential conflicts with institutional interests. Furthermore, we examine the impact of conducting maternity research with refugee populations, which can shed light on hospital services but may require careful handling to avoid diluting the richness and complexity of the data. We also discuss strategies for interviewing powerful groups and the importance of considering social and cultural aspects. In doing so, we emphasise the ethical dimensions and the implications for the research outcomes beyond the academic realm.

The supervisor or mentor /colleague can be used to discuss balancing institutional concerns and research integrity. When researchers wish to study at their school or university, ethical dilemmas may arise if detrimental issues come to light that the institution wishes to suppress. Navigating such situations demands a delicate balance between research integrity and the potential repercussions on the institution. Researchers must carefully consider how to handle sensitive findings to ensure transparency while protecting the participants and maintaining a commitment to truth and objectivity.

When researching in a refuge or in the community I found a very moving topic that triggered my child protection drives, Ethnography and Maternity Research with Refugees.

Ethnographic studies focused on maternity experiences among refugee populations can yield valuable insights. However, such research might uncover shortcomings in maternity services, potentially implicating the institution. The challenge lies in presenting an authentic representation of the experiences without watering down the richness and complexity of the data to safeguard institutional interests.

Ethnography provides a platform to amplify marginalised voices, including those of refugee women. However, accessing and interviewing powerful groups, such as medical professionals in maternity research, requires thoughtful strategies. Researchers must navigate power dynamics, ensure balanced representation, and seek perspectives from various stakeholders to present a comprehensive view. This aspect is not in this research book nor is interviewing schools, but it has been discussed and is a missing strand of research in Coventry.

Being a non-government organisation, The Carriers of Hope are in a very good position for exploring social and cultural considerations of the many refugee families that are our clients.

Ethnographic research calls for a keen understanding of social and cultural contexts and by running tegular groups to give away food, furniture, clothing and play opportunities the clint group can be seen and spoken with. Researchers must be attentive to the intricacies of their study communities, acknowledging the influence of cultural norms and societal structures on the participants' experiences.

The significance of ethnographic research extends beyond academic discussions. Such studies can drive positive change by uncovering the realities of people's lived experiences. However, researchers must recognise that influencing powerful groups and societal structures is a complex undertaking, and the implications of their research reach far beyond academia.

Conclusion

Ethnography within institutional settings is a multifaceted endeavour that demands careful navigation of ethical considerations, institutional interests, and research integrity. Researchers must be attentive to the power dynamics involved, especially when studying marginalised communities like refugees. The impact of their work can extend beyond academic discourse, making it crucial to approach ethnographic research with a conscientious and ethical lens. Ultimately, striking a balance between objectivity and sensitivity can lead to impactful research that contributes to a deeper understanding of diverse lived experiences and fosters positive societal change.

17 RESEARCH PLANNING AND SUPERVISION

Organising an essay into clear sections is crucial for maintaining a coherent and logical structure. I teach methods according to what my student needs. For dyslexic students, writing in boxes and separating each section helps them. Several effective ways can be used to ensure academic essay organisation. Here are some strategies and tools you can employ to achieve a well-structured essay but do find your unique way of teaching yourself or others.

Create an outline before starting the writing process. An outline serves as a roadmap, helping you determine the main sections and their subtopics. It provides a clear structure for your essay and covers all relevant points. This also helps to see if the essay is balanced with enough research ideas in every section.

Although the introduction comes first in every essay, it can be written last. Begin with an engaging introduction that provides context and captures the reader's attention. Clearly state your thesis or main argument, guiding the rest of your essay.

Next, the writer must create the body paragraphs. Divide the body of your essay into logical sections, with each section focusing on a specific aspect or supporting point related to your thesis. Use topic sentences at the beginning of each paragraph to introduce the main idea and provide evidence or examples to support your claims. The notion of sticking to the essay title is lost for some writers, so this does have to be taught.

The study skills modules in university often include a page of "Transition words" Utilise transition words and phrases to create smooth connections between paragraphs and sections. Transition words like "however," "moreover," "on the other hand," "in addition to," and "conversely" help maintain coherence and guide the reader through the essay.

I always teach students to PEE. They must start with a point and then reference or find evidence about that point. They end the section by expanding what they have written, usually applying it to their question or essay title. Many students ask, "How many references should I have?". It is about referencing every time there is a sweeping or unsubstantiated statement. I teach students to put the line they wrote into Google Scholar to see if anything is written about the issue. This is a sure-fire way of finding appropriate reading and checking that the writing is from good evidence rather than just made up.

Sometimes I insert sub-headings with the student so they can see how we can classify information and theme it into sections. The purpose is to teach a method to unscramble the writing and ensure the writer can decide on the flow of ideas. We can remove the subheadings and put in linking words that finish off the section and introduce the next section. If appropriate for the essay type and length, incorporate subheadings within the body paragraphs to further organise your content. Subheadings help break down complex topics, clarify, and enhance readability. Students can learn this using different colours to underline each issue in subsequent essays. Some dyslexic learners print off their script and cut it into sections, then rewrite it all to try and make sense of organisation. This takes so much time and energy that I teach different ways that are as effective for students.

The topic that most students find hard at first is evidence and analysis, and this scores the highest grades. The skilled writer can ensure that each section balances evidence and research. Critical teaching is about presenting supporting evidence such as facts, data, quotes, or examples, and then how to analyse and interpret that evidence to demonstrate its relevance and how it supports the thesis. This is often done by tutors in the presentation in class, but very innovative ways can be designed so students try analysing data for themselves. The fact that any old reference is stuck at the end of a sentence means the student needs help to apply what they have read to their work.

Another area for improvement is the conclusion. The assignment brief may state, "Conclude your essay by summarising the main points and concisely restating the thesis. Avoid introducing new information in conclusion ".

Instead, I teach the student to emphasise the significance of their argument and leave the reader with a lasting impression. This discussion usually leaves the student satisfied that they said something exciting or original and can increase their pride and identity as a writer.

The most challenging area for a student is often proofreading because they have produced and wordsmithed the work they read and what needs to be added. Some students choose family members with poor literacy skills to do this for them. I always advise "cold reading" as the first thing in the morning when the brain can be more accurate. Proofreading and editing is a skill that needs to be taught at university, but usually it is not, it is just recommended. Telling students, "After writing your essay, review it carefully to check for coherence, clarity, and overall structure." is only helpful instruction if they know what a good structure is and if they have made coherent points. It is worth a practice with examples from the student's writing.

Extra grades are available if a writer can ensure that each section flows logically into the next and that arguments are well-supported and coherent. It can be taught, and students can use proofreading tools like Grammarly or enlist the help of peers or mentors for feedback.

The essay's specific structure and organisation may vary depending on the subject, assignment guidelines, and essay type. I always refer to any detailed instructions from the instructor or academic institution. The student might paste them into the script until that section is finished. The instructions are best decoded and highlighted to keep the writer on course.

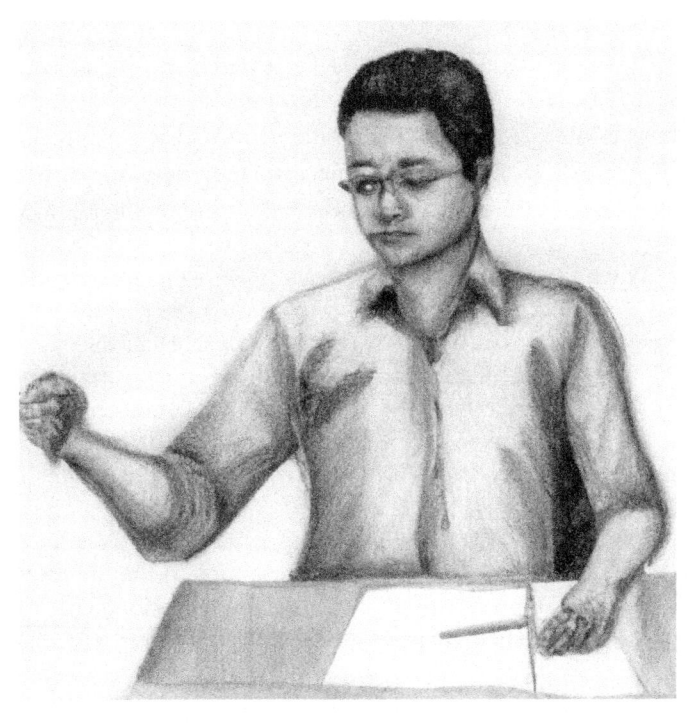

Organising a Solid Research Outline - Example of a Writing Frame
The Challenges Faced by Pregnant Women in the Asylum System
Introduction
- The legal definitions and distinctions between asylum seekers and refugees in the U.K.
- Asylum seekers have fled their country and applied for asylum in the U.K.
- Refugees meet the criteria of the 1951 Refugee Convention and have legal permission to stay in the country.
- Highlight the delays in the decision-making process, leaving asylum seekers in limbo.

Background
- The researcher's biases and background.
- Vulnerability of migrant groups, including refused asylum seekers, trafficked people, undocumented migrants, pregnant women, and children.
- Pregnant women seek asylum as a vulnerable group with specific health and well-being concerns.
- Studies show poor experiences of asylum seekers in the U.K. due to unmet health and social care needs.

Challenges Faced by Pregnant Asylum Seekers
- Asylum seekers experience isolation, homelessness, and poverty.
- Difficulties in accessing adequate community care, including language barriers and need for interpreters.
- Impact of entitlement checks and forms on accessing necessary services.
- Late and inadequate antenatal care poses risks to women and unborn children.
- Reports of vulnerable asylum seekers placed in hotels without proper support during the COVID-19 pandemic.

Conclusion
- Summary of the distinctions between asylum seekers and refugees in the U.K.
- Challenges faced by pregnant women within the asylum system include limited access to healthcare and support.
- Acknowledgement of the unique situation of the research group due to COVID-19 restrictions.

After /during the research; The Research Group and Context
- Participants are well-informed about their entitlements and access information.
- Support from Coventry's asylum support officer, migrant help, and charity networks.
- Participants were housed with other new mothers but were restricted from leaving due to COVID-19.

You can also organise your whole thesis and put in dates to meet your supervisor and carry out the research in a Gantt chart.

The Gantt chart is a project management tool that visually represents a project's schedule over time. It was developed by Henry Gantt, an American engineer and management consultant, in the early 20th century.

Henry Gantt created the Gantt chart in the 1910s to improve project planning and scheduling in industrial settings, particularly during the construction of ships and buildings. His diagrams were initially drawn on large sheets of paper, and he used them to track the progress of projects, allocate resources, and manage tasks efficiently.

The Gantt chart consists of horizontal bars representing individual tasks or activities in a project and a time axis that shows the project's timeline. Each bar's length corresponds to the duration of the job, and the bars are arranged sequentially based on the project's planned order of execution. This way, project managers can easily visualise the project's overall timeline, identify dependencies between tasks, and determine the critical path for timely completion.

Today, Gantt charts are widely used in various industries and are often created using project management software. They have become essential for project managers and team members to plan, track, and manage projects effectively, ensuring that tasks are completed on time and within the allocated resources.

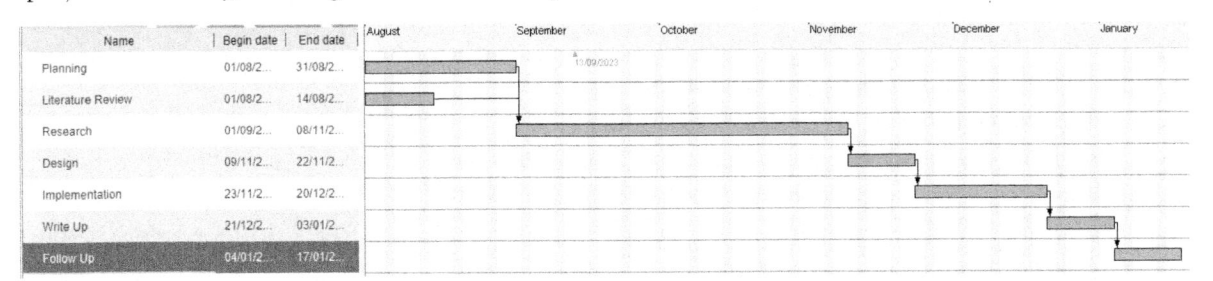

Name	Begin date	End date
Planning	01/08/2...	31/08/2...
Literature Review	01/08/2...	14/08/2...
Research	01/09/2...	08/11/2...
Design	09/11/2...	22/11/2...
Implementation	23/11/2...	20/12/2...
Write Up	21/12/2...	03/01/2...
Follow Up	04/01/2...	17/01/2...

Google search has hundreds of Gantt charts and your librarian or technical help at university can design one with you.

Ensuring Effective Communication with Your Supervisor for Academic Progress

In the pursuit of academic excellence, it is essential to maintain a constructive relationship with your supervisor. However, there may be instances where your supervisor still needs to review your submissions, despite your considerable investment in your course. This article outlines practical steps to effectively organise and engage with your supervisor to establish an explicit agreement about expectations and ensure productive supervision meetings. To maximise the benefits of your supervision:

- Open communication for expectations alignment:
- Begin by fostering open communication with your supervisor.
- Initiate a conversation to clarify your mutual expectations.
- Emphasise the importance of regular feedback on your work, as it forms the foundation of your academic progress.
- Request Commitment to Review Your Work:

During your discussion, seek a clear commitment from your supervisor to review your submissions diligently. A written agreement will help reinforce this commitment and provide you with a reference point in case any issues arise.

Enhance Productive Supervision Meetings:

Highlight the significance of your work being read before your supervision meetings. Stress that these meetings are most valuable when both parties thoroughly engage with the material. Emphasise the need for timely feedback, enabling you to incorporate valuable insights into your research.

Avoid Wasting Time in the Initial Years:

Early in your academic journey, it is crucial to avoid wasting time. Express your concern about the potential loss of two years of progress due to a lack of guidance. Seek assurances that your supervisor will actively guide your research from the beginning.

Seek Guidance on Fieldwork:

If your research involves fieldwork, discuss your plans with your supervisor. Seek advice on refining your fieldwork approach to ensure its relevance and effectiveness in achieving your research objectives.

Raise Concerns and Seek Help:

Don't hesitate to bring up any concerns or uncertainties you may have regarding your research or methodology. Supervisors are there to assist and provide guidance, so make the most of this opportunity to receive their valuable input.

Expect Punctuality and Respect:

Maintain a professional tone while expecting punctuality and respect from your supervisor. Show your dedication to the research process and expect the same level of commitment in return.

Effective organisation and communication with your supervisor are vital for a successful academic journey. By establishing clear expectations and securing a commitment to timely feedback, you can make the most of your supervision and progress confidently in your research. Remember that open dialogue and respectful collaboration are key to maximising the benefits of your PhD program and achieving academic excellence.

Supervising a Student's Work
To supervise students' research papers using the provided headings, you can follow these guidelines:
- Emphasise the importance of outlining in the research and writing process, explaining how it helps organise thoughts and ideas.
- Clarify the research outline's purpose as a roadmap to structure the essay and guide the research process.
- Highlight the significance of balance and coherence in the outline to ensure a well-organised and cohesive research paper.

For the first session I use a roll of wallpaper to section off the chapters. Then as ideas are discussed I show the student which chapter they will write about the research thesis in . As they sort out their methods and conceptual frameworks, they can see how it is built through the work in order and how it flows. This first session helps the student to have faith in what they are proposing and to ask basic questions about the work.

A main issue for a supervisor is to seek the ideas from the student and not to impose their own ideas so the student develops an understanding the purpose of an outline. The function of an outline and how it serves as a blueprint for the paper's structure can be shown visually as ideas are added to the wallpaper. Each chapter is affected by the others so the whole workflows. The outline is kept for further use such as improving organisation and time management. An outline enhances clarity and keeps the research focused on the main objectives and it reminds the supervisor and student of the research objectives. If the objectives change easily the strong flow will be disrupted and the student can loose their way and waste time and efforts.

An experienced supervisor can see a view of the research that is presented and help to instruct a student in the elements of an effective research outline:

They do not waste effort re directing the student over and over and they can give better feedback. Good supervisors stress the importance of a clear thesis statement in the outline to provide a central focus for the research paper. They ensure the focus does not become wishy washy as the work continues. They can guide students on identifying the main sections of the paper and the specific objectives they aim to achieve. By having clarity designed on the overall wallpaper roll the good supervisor can help students understand the process of determining the scope and depth of each subtopic to maintain a coherent structure.

A good supervisor can work right from day one on structuring the research outline. They can, due to their experience in the area of study ,break down the components of the introduction section, including the hook, background information, and thesis statement.

In follow up supervisions the supervisor can guide students in structuring the body section with well-defined main areas and relevant subtopics. A big issue for new researchers is the organisation of a thesis themes. The writing academically is often new to students and they have to review some of their work with the supervisor to find a point, some evidence to back it up and a personal analysis .The skilled supervisor can advise on organising the conclusion section to effectively summarise key findings and restate the thesis while offering a closing remark. In this way the PhD or degree is a course of learning how to write and use analytical literacies.

Another skill of an experienced supervisor is to teach how to ensure balance and coherence in the outline that will then develop into a balanced thesis. I always encourage students to assess the distribution of research ideas across the sections to avoid information overload in some areas and neglect in others. Most of the time the task is to narrow down the research, to focus on fewer subtopics. I Stress the importance of verifying that subtopics are relevant and contribute meaningfully to the essay's overall focus.

Some feedback is done with the student when discussing their written work and I help students establish smooth transitions between main sections to maintain flow and logical progression in the paper. Many students do not know how to summarise or round up their section or sub section.

In helping the students seek help from peers and colleagues' future support is included in their journey. I Advise students to seek feedback from peers or instructors to gain different perspectives on the outline's clarity and organisation.

Feedback is never just written because this can strike fear into students, so we discuss how to revise and reorganise the outline based on feedback and their critical assessment.

I always emphasise the significance of finalising the outline before starting the writing process to ensure a well-structured research paper or thesis.

In conclusion the first session I always show the significance of outlining as a fundamental tool in guiding the research and writing journey.

We use the outline and change or add ideas to make an outline for each chapter ensuring the student gets the importance of balance and coherence in the outline for a comprehensive and logically structured research paper.

Leveraging Your Supervisor's Support for Academic Progress and Engagement

Supervisors are pivotal in shaping students' success in pursuing advanced degrees. Beyond reviewing submissions, they can offer valuable assistance in various aspects of academic life. This article explores how supervisors can provide support, from mock vivas and presentations to identifying robust debates within your field. Additionally, it addresses the issue of students who lack feedback, emphasising the significance of utilising the supervisor's expertise to overcome feelings of isolation.

Mock Vivas and Presentations:

Your supervisor can be an invaluable resource when preparing for vital academic milestones, such as vivas and presentations. By conducting mock vivas, they can help you anticipate and address potential questions and challenges. This practice enhances your confidence and equips you to deliver a polished and well-structured presentation.

Writing Publications:

Navigating the world of academic publishing can be daunting, especially for early-career researchers. Supervisors with publishing experience can guide you through the process, from choosing suitable journals to crafting impactful manuscripts. Their mentorship can significantly improve the quality and visibility of your work.

Identifying Robust Debates:

In any academic field, robust debates contribute to intellectual growth and advancement. With their extensive knowledge, your supervisor can help you identify critical debates within your subject area. These discussions will expand your understanding and position your research within the broader academic discourse.

Combating Isolation:

Many students worldwide struggle with a lack of feedback and support, leading to feelings of isolation in their academic journey. You can overcome this sense of loneliness by maintaining open lines of communication with your supervisor. Regular meetings and constructive feedback foster a supportive environment where you can share ideas and seek guidance.

Supervisors are not only tasked with evaluating academic progress; they are invaluable mentors capable of offering multifaceted support. From assisting with mock vivas and presentations to guiding you through publishing endeavours and highlighting significant debates in your field, their expertise is indispensable. By actively engaging with your supervisor and leveraging their mentorship, you can confidently navigate your academic journey and conquer the challenges that come your way. Remember that communication and collaboration with your supervisor are key to transforming a potentially lonely and daunting experience into a rewarding and enriching academic pursuit.

Keeping Supervision Notes

The university does need to keep records of your supervision but many, due to workload will do a very light touch and forget when you did what. I personally kept my own notes and could identify if they redirected me telling me one thing and then another. The student is usually asked what you did this year, and the supervisor makes their notes from that to decide if the student can go through to another year. One of the problems is what notes should be kept and how deep should they be? The following is just an idea and often tutors are time poor and supervise so many students so need the student to be prepared.

Supervision Notes Template for Research Student

[Date of Supervision Meeting: _____]
Student Information:
- Name:
- Research Topic:
- Degree Program:
- Date of Enrolment:

Supervisor Information:
- Name:
- Department/Institution:

Agenda for the Meeting:
- Research Progress:
    - Overview of progress made since the last meeting.
    - Accomplishments and milestones achieved.
    - Challenges encountered and how they were addressed.
- Research Objectives and Timeline:
    - Review and discuss the overall research objectives.
    - Assess progress towards meeting specific goals and deadlines.
    - Update or modify the research timeline if necessary.
- Data Collection and Analysis:
    - Discuss data collection methods and sources.
    - Review the status of data collection and any potential issues.
    - Consider the data analysis approach and its alignment with the research questions.
- Literature Review:
    - Recap the key findings from the recent literature review.
    - Identify gaps and areas for further exploration.
    - Discuss the integration of new literature into the research.
- Methodology and Research Design:
    - Verify the appropriateness of the chosen research design.
    - Review any changes or modifications to the methodology.
    - Ensure alignment between research questions and preferred methods.
- Ethical Considerations:
    - Confirm adherence to ethical guidelines and protocols.
    - Discuss any ethical challenges encountered and their resolution.
- Results and Findings:
    - Share any preliminary findings or results.
    - Analyse the significance and implications of the findings.
    - Determine the next steps for data analysis and interpretation.

- Academic Writing and Organisation:
  - Review the structure and organisation of the research paper or thesis.
  - Offer feedback on writing clarity, coherence, and language.
  - Discuss strategies for improving academic writing skills.
- Resources and Support:
  - Identify any additional help or support required.
  - Discuss opportunities for conference presentations or publication.
- Action Plan:
  - Establish specific action items for the student to work on before the next meeting.
  - Set deadlines for the completion of each task.
  - Clarify the supervisor's role in providing support and feedback.
- Any Other Business:
  - Address any additional topics or concerns related to the research project.
  - Discuss future meeting schedules and expectations.

Action Items for the Next Meeting:
- [List specific action items agreed upon during the meeting]

Supervisor's Remarks:
- [Include any additional comments or suggestions for the student's research progress]

Student's Remarks:
- [Provide the student's response to the feedback and action items]

Next Meeting Date:
- [Agree on the date and time for the next supervision meeting]

Signature:
- [Supervisor's signature]
- [Student's signature]

Note: This template is a general guideline for taking supervision notes for research students. Feel free to modify and adapt it to suit your requirements and preferences.

18 CITIZENS SOCIAL RESEARCH

Motherhood by Migena
Abstract
The emotional aspects of living in a shared house were described much more than poverty. The women aspired and dreams of gaining a decision from the home office or moving to see family. Their depression and stress were attributed to the living conditions of others in the house!

Having a baby for the first time also can be very stressful because some of the women have mental health issues, so their moods are always up and down!

Also, the other thing I could get from this research was the beautiful moments when I asked some of the ladies about their babies! How much emotion they talked about them and the feeling of being a mother!

Introduction
Citizen social science is the term most associated with a form of citizen science in the social sciences or, alternatively, one that focuses on the social aspects of citizen science. It can involve citizens in designing or conducting social research, such as ideation, analysis, data collection and impact. (Albert 2021)

Citizen science, also known as volunteer monitoring, is described as public participation in scientific research. This work results from the Coventry Citizen Science course Coventry University ran in April 2021. I was taking part in the course, and this is my research. My bias is that I am an asylum-seeking woman who has just had her first baby and lives in the refuge where I have interviewed other mummies. Many of the participants are my friends. The good thing is that they will give me interviews that they may not give to outsiders. The Home Office sends pregnant women to the refuge; the 20 women can stay here until their baby is one year old.

Methods
Peer research is a participatory method in which people with lived experience of the issues being studied participate in directing and conducting the research.

It aims to move away from the 'extractive' model of social research and to empower people to affect positive change by participating in research on their communities(https://icstudies.org.uk)

"Like other participatory methods, peer research recognises that individuals within any community being researched are themselves competent agents, capable of participating in research on various levels, including as researchers. "(Wadsworth 1998)

Peer researchers use their lived experience and contextual understanding of a social or geographical community to help generate information about their peers for research purposes. They may assist with research design, developing research tools, collecting and analysing data or writing up and disseminating findings.

Peer research can also be referred to as 'service user' research when it is conducted together with the users of a specific service to evaluate that service.

The data was created by the ladies that live in the refuge. I asked them interview questions.

Questions/interview

Motherhood (asylum seeker, mums being for the first time)

Before I start with questions, I will record just the voice to take notes! Also, if you don't want to answer any questions, skip! If you agree, let's start the interview!

1. How did you react when you discovered you were becoming a mother?
2. How did you react when you saw your baby for the first time?
3. What was the first word you said to the baby when it was born?
4. How hard do you find being a mum as an asylum seeker?
5. Did you have any friends or families from the moment you gave birth? (In case they are alone) How did you feel doing all this on your own?
6. Do you find time to take care of yourself?
7. Can you describe what is your baby for you?
8. What is the biggest wish for your baby? What is your biggest dream?

Questionnaires are possible during the COVID-19 pandemic because I live with the ladies. They enable people to take their time, think about it, and return to the questionnaire later. Participants can state their views or feelings privately without worrying about the possible reaction of the researcher. Unfortunately, some people may still be inclined to try to give socially acceptable answers. People should be encouraged to answer the questions as honestly as possible to avoid the researchers drawing false conclusions from the study.

Also, the CSS course required me to read something about the topic before I made up the questions. The research I've chosen is with the ladies (mums for the first time) who have already gone through emotional trauma as asylum seekers. In social science terms, ethics are to protect the participants and the researcher. The negative impact of research on people is well documented, so I put the search terms "asylum-seeking new mothers" into Google Scholar.

I found a lot about if asylum seekers could qualify for money. Still, one good paper from the British Medical Journal by Gewalt et al. (2019) said asylum-seeking new mums are highly vulnerable and have special needs, but there is very little research done about this. So, my research will add to the knowledge about motherhood. This writing by Gewalt focused on material needs and poverty due to no money, poor hygiene, poor housing, and no food, which led to health difficulties for asylum seekers. The reading also showed women in this position to have poor mental health, and their babies were poorly and often died.

Analysis of Data

The ladies chose what to disclose, and I recorded only the voice (without showing their faces or any part of their bodies).

The answers could have been presented as one case study, or I could theme the answers. A case study looks like this when I take all the answers to each question and then round up a point at the end.

1. *I was very excited when I learnt I was pregnant.*
2. *I cried. I couldn't believe he was mine*
3. *I told my baby I love him.*
4. *I find it very hard being a mum as an asylum seeker because I must rely on charities and the Home Office for my baby's upkeep, and I am not certain how long it will take to get a decision from the Home Office about if I can stay*

in the UK. It's very stressful.
5. *I had no friends or family when I gave birth, but I was not alone because the surgeon requested a very kind lady from the maternity department to be with me and hold my hand.*
6. *I am always very busy with the baby and have very little time for myself even having a proper shower is a problem because I must wait for my baby to sleep. I can only have 10 minutes shower in case my baby wakes up, and I am not in the room.*
7. *My biggest wish is for my baby to be always healthy, grow up to be respectful, loving and have better opportunities.*
8. *My biggest dream is for my baby to accomplish what God created him to accomplish and be among people who make this world a better place*

So all of the mummies were grateful for their babies even though they were in a difficult place. These asylum seekers' pregnancy and motherhood journey has been filled with emotions, challenges, and hopes. The excitement upon learning about the pregnancy and the overwhelming joy when the baby arrived is evident in their words. However, being an asylum seeker has introduced unique difficulties, as the individual must rely on charities and the Home Office for their baby's well-being, uncertain about their future in the UK.

Despite not having friends or family during childbirth, they found comfort and support from a compassionate lady in the maternity department. However, being a new mother brings challenges, leaving little time for self-care and personal needs.

Throughout these experiences, the asylum seeker's primary focus remains on their baby's well-being and future. Their deepest wishes revolve around their child's health, happiness, and success. They aspire for their baby to grow up to be a respectful, loving individual with better opportunities, capable of positively impacting the world.

In this story of motherhood, we witness resilience, love, and a strong desire to provide the best for their child despite the challenges posed by their asylum-seeking status. It exemplifies many asylum-seeking mothers' strength and determination as they navigate the complexities of raising their children in a new and uncertain environment.

The data collected gave critical themes, presenting these rather than identifying individual contributors. The reader could then see many similarities between the answers from every case of a woman describing motherhood in a refuge `as an asylum seeker.

Participants

The research method is a case study of a refugee with 20 asylum seekers women who have just become moms for the first time!

Ethical considerations

The discussions about ethics were online on our "What's App" group and in private conversations with each woman who agreed to be questioned. The qualitative data collection does need to be reliable as I can get it, and creating reliable results starts from designing the interview.

Research ethics are the moral principles governing how researchers should conduct their work. These principles shape research regulations agreed upon by groups such as university governing bodies, communities, or governments. All researchers should follow any regulations that apply to their work. This research will not lead to direct changes for the ladies I am interviewing, so I will not promise any gains for their participation.

It is important to adhere to ethical norms in research for several reasons. First, norms promote research aims, such as knowledge, truth, and error avoidance. For example, prohibitions against fabricating, falsifying, or misrepresenting research data promote the truth and minimise error.

I understood and used ethical procedures even though they were my friends. They include.

- Respect for persons – autonomy and protecting
- Beneficence and non-maleficence

- Justice
- Informed consent
- Confidentiality and data protection
- Integrity

Results

1. How did you react when you discovered you were becoming a mother?

Interestingly, no one meant to be pregnant; they found out as a surprise.

Person 1: It was a very confusing feeling. I didn't know what to do. I felt wired.
Person 2: When I found out I was pregnant, I felt so emotional I started crying.
Person 3: I would like to skip this question.
Person 4: I cried a lot, and the first thing I thought was to be a boy!
Person 5: I was so happy because I was so sad in those times.
Person6: I cried, and I smiled at the same time!
Person7: I cannot describe how emotional it was!
Person 8: the best feeling ever!
Person 9: Actually, it happened by accident, but when I found out I was pregnant, I thanked God because my dream was coming true!
Person10: So so emotional, couldn't wait to find out the gender!

So being pregnant was not all good news to everyone at first, but it was very emotional for all because we were in the situation of being away from family, so we knew it would be something we do alone. The reactions of these individuals upon discovering they were becoming mothers reveal a range of emotions and circumstances. The common thread is that the pregnancies were unexpected, catching them by surprise. Some reactions were confused, while others were marked by intense emotions, leading to tears and mixed feelings.

Person 3's reluctance to answer the question might suggest a complex emotional response or personal reasons they prefer not to disclose. On the other hand, Person 8's description of it as the "best feeling ever" implies an overwhelming sense of joy and happiness.

The diversity of emotions, including feelings of happiness, sadness, confusion, gratitude, and excitement, highlights the complex nature of the journey to motherhood. Each person's unique experience showcases the deeply personal and transformative impact of discovering one's pregnancy.

Overall, this collection of responses reflects the diverse and individualised emotional experiences that come with the revelation of impending motherhood. It demonstrates that becoming a mother is a deeply personal and significant event that can elicit many emotions and reactions, making each woman's journey to motherhood uniquely special.

2. How did you react when you saw your baby for the first time?

Person 1: I just cried so much.
Person 2: I cried and laughed because I had never seen such a beautiful baby!
Person 3: I just cried a lot!
Person 4: I just cried! I couldn't believe that!
Person 5: I felt so emotional!
Person 6: it was my first time crying with happiness!
Person 7: I would like to skip the question; I feel so emotional right now!
Person 8: I couldn't believe that I just become a mother!
Person 9: my only biggest dream was on my chest; what emotion was to hold all the world in my hands!

Person 10: I tried a feeling that I never had tried before! I couldn't stop hugging and kissing her! I didn't want to leave her even a second with someone else!

For all the women having a baby was a very emotional thing. These reactions demonstrate the diverse and individualised nature of emotional responses to the discovery of pregnancy. They range from confusion, mixed emotions, and overwhelming joy to gratitude and eagerness. The reactions also hint at the significance of this life-changing moment and the complex feelings that accompany the journey to motherhood. Becoming a mother is a deeply personal and transformative experience that elicits a wide range of emotions, reflecting the uniqueness of each person's path to motherhood.

3. What was the first word you said to the baby when it was born?

Person 1: God bless you!
Person 2: Welcome, my miracle; I hope you have a long and wonderful life.
Person 3: Welcome, my baby boy!
Person 4: God bless you, my little man!
Person 5: Welcome, my little one! Thank you for giving me the most beautiful name in this world! Mummy!
Person 6: The first thing that I said was, " omg she's so beautiful, sooo gorgeous, and so tiny "
Person 7: I said finally, you are here, I love you!
Person 8: I thank God for the best gift ever!
Person 9: I started to cry; I couldn't believe that I thanked God because I couldn't ask for more!
Person 10: welcome, my beautiful baby!

Analysing these quotes from new asylum-seeking mummies, we can observe the following themes and emotions:

Blessings and Gratitude: Several individuals express blessings and gratitude to God for the baby's arrival. They view the child as a precious gift and feel thankful for their presence.

Joy and Excitement: There is a strong sense of joy and excitement in welcoming the new-born. Words like "miracle," "beautiful," "gorgeous," and "tiny" reflect the happiness and delight experienced by the mothers.

Love and Affection: Love and affection are evident in the quotes as the mothers use endearing terms like "my baby boy," "my little man," "my little one," and "my beautiful baby." They express deep emotional connections to their newborns.

Overwhelming Emotions: The baby's arrival brings overwhelming emotions for some mothers. Person 9 mentions crying in disbelief and feeling immensely grateful to God for the precious gift they've received.

Sense of Fulfilment: The mothers convey a sense of fulfilment and completion in their lives with the arrival of their babies. They refer to their child as the "most beautiful name in this world" and the "best gift ever."

Eager Anticipation: Person 7's quote suggests a period of anticipation before the baby's arrival, possibly indicating a long and challenging journey leading to the moment.

Overall, the quotes showcase the immense joy, love, and gratitude experienced by asylum-seeking mothers upon the arrival of their babies. The language reflects a deep emotional bond and a sense of hope for a bright future for the mothers and their newborns.

4. How hard do you find being a mum as an asylum seeker?

For many reasons, it is difficult to be a mother for the first time as an asylum seeker! Many women feel so sad that their baby does not have the best start; they cannot provide what they want.

Person 1: It is difficult because I'm alone. I don't have any people to help me, and I have to take care of my baby despite all my difficulties. It is also difficult for me because it is a new country, language, and people!

Person2: So so difficult! Being all alone in a new country and having nothing ready for the baby was really hard!
Person 3: oh dear, it is so hard! Can't describe how hard it is!
Person 4: oh my God, I think this is the worst thing in my life!
Person 5: it's so hard being an asylum seeker, especially when you have a baby who doesn't completely deserve to be on these conditions!
Person 6: it's so difficult because I can't offer my baby what I wish for!
Person7: being an asylum seeker its hard but being an asylum seeker and a mum simultaneously is difficult!
Person 8 it's soooo sooo hard, because you are under the same roof with too many people, and we don't have the basic stuff to live!
Person 9: Being in a shared accommodation is okay sometimes because like this, you are always surrounded by different people! But I can say that being a mom like an asylum seeker it's very hard! You are always panicking and waiting for a long time to get a decision from the Home Office!
Person10: life is hard for some people, much harder for us, asylum seeker mums! Horrible!

Only one person had their partner with them for the labour, some had friends, and to some, they needed to have their phone to contact family. Overall, these reactions showcase the profound emotional impact of witnessing the birth of their baby for the first time. Crying is a common response, along with joy, disbelief, happiness, and a sense of fulfilment. The descriptions reflect the transformational nature of becoming a parent and the overwhelming love and connection towards their newborns. This life-changing moment is filled with emotions that are difficult to understand fully. Still, each response captures the unique and powerful experience of seeing their baby for the first time.

5. Did you have any friends or families in the moment you gave birth? (In case they are alone) How did you feel doing all this on your own?

Person 1: I was so lucky because, during my pregnancy, I had the opportunity to know a wonderful person who was an asylum seeker like me! She helped me a lot!
Person 2: I didn't have anybody to help me out!
I was all alone! But I did well!
Person 3: I had my friends around, which helped me for a few days when I gave birth!
Person 4: I had some friends but not nearby; they came the first days I gave birth. For any worries I had during the baby's growth, I spoke to my family via WhatsApp.
Person 5: I was all alone! The friends I had was far away from me! During my birth, I was just the midwife and nurse!
Person 6: I had some friends who helped me!
Person 7: I had a family member who helped me out!
Person 8: I was all alone, on my way, without nobody near me! I just got a friend, but she was far away!
Person 9: I had my partner with me during the labour!
Person 10: I had a friend who came when I was in labour!

Overall, the responses show a range of support systems or lack of them for asylum seekers during pregnancy and childbirth. Some had close friends or family members who assisted, while others experienced feelings of isolation and relied on medical professionals for support. It highlights the importance of social connections and support networks for individuals going through such significant life events. The variations in experiences also underscore asylum seekers' unique challenges during this crucial phase of their lives.

6. Do you find time to take care of yourself?
The mothers often have time to take care of themselves when the baby sleeps a lot, but as the baby becomes more active, it is harder.

Person 1: Haha, you are kidding!
Person 2: now my baby is one year old, so it's becoming hard to find time for myself but I can't say I'm not taking care of myself!
Person 3: yes, of course, my baby is a big boy now.
Person 4: not usually, my baby cries a lot, and sometimes I don't have time even to cook!
person 5: yes, I try my best to find some free time to care for myself.
Person6: my baby is little, so I had to look after him every minute, but I also can manage to take care of myself.
Person 7: I started to feed my baby, and now I don't have a lot of time for me!
Person 8: Sometimes
Person 9: I can do both; look after me and my baby at the same time.
Person 10: yes, sometimes, for example, when I need to brush my teeth or shower, the ladies in the house look after my baby!

These quotes show new mothers' various challenges and strategies to balance caring for their babies and finding time for self-care. Some mothers find it more manageable as their babies grow older, while others struggle due to the demands of caring for a young infant. Some rely on help from others, while others do their best to multitask and manage themselves and their babies simultaneously. The responses show new mothers' diverse experiences and priorities when it comes to taking care of themselves amid the responsibilities of motherhood.

7. Can you describe what is your baby for you?
All of the mothers are able to be emotional and joyful about their babies.

Person 1: it is very difficult to describe how a feel about my daughter. She's my world, my future. She's the only reason why I live!
Person 2: I feel so emotional when somebody asks me about this question, so I prefer to skip it.
Person 3: my son is my world, my king, my biggest love !
Person 4: the words aren't enough to describe what my son is to me !
Person 5: my daughter is the best thing that happened in my life , she's my best friend and I love her so much!
Person 6: my son is my everything, which is why i smile!
Person 7: My baby is my universe!
Person 8: my daughter, my biggest dream!
Person 9: my son is everything to me, thank god for this beautiful gift!
Person 10: my baby is my breath; she's the only one I got!

The data showcases the deep emotional bond between these parents and their children. The children are cherished, loved, and held in the highest regard, with each parent finding profound meaning and purpose in their relationship with their sons and daughters. These expressions of love reflect parenthood's incredible impact on shaping and enriching their lives, making their children an integral part of who they are and what they hold most dear.

8. What is the biggest wish for your baby? What is your biggest dream?
All of the ladies wanted good futures for their first baby.

Person 1: I wish the best for my daughter and to be healthy!
My biggest dream is to offer a good life for my daughter and to make her happy!
Person 2: I wish for my baby to have a good life, that's also my biggest dream!
Person 3: I wish to see my baby growing like he deserves to; my biggest dream is to see him happy!
Person 4: I want my little girl to be happy, to see her smile always. My biggest dream is just her!

Person 5: I want my son to be a gentleman and to know how to respect women! My biggest dream is to see him grow in the best way!

Person 6: I wish my baby to be good and healthy. My biggest dream? Hmmm , already came true; my son is here with me!

Person 7: I want my baby to smile every second of his life!

Person 8: my biggest dream is to see my daughter growing up and being a "powerful woman " in the future!

Person 9: I want to offer my baby the best life I never had! I want her to be as happy as possible, and I wish that the Home Office to get the decision as soon as possible so I can start preparing for my daughter's life!

Person 10: I want him to be happy and healthy. That's all I wish!

The research data reveals the deep love and devotion these parents have for their children, as evidenced by their heartfelt wishes and dreams. Their aspirations revolve around ensuring their children's well-being, happiness, and success, illustrating the importance they place on their roles as parents. The parents' desires to provide a good life, happiness, health, and positive values reflect their commitment to nurturing and guiding their children toward a bright and fulfilling future.

This collection of responses showcases the universal nature of parental aspirations, as parents from diverse backgrounds share the goal of wanting the best for their children. The data demonstrates the power of parental love and the selfless nature of parenthood, where the well-being and happiness of their children become the central focus of their hopes and dreams.

References

Albert A., Balázs B., Butkevičienė E., Mayer K., Perelló J. (2021) Citizen Social Science: New and Established Approaches to Participation in Social Research. In: Vohland K. et al. (eds) The Science of Citizen Science. Springer, Cham. https://doi.org/10.1007/978-3-030-58278-4_7

Gewalt, ‚S, Berger, S.,Szecsenyi J., & Bozorgmehr Z. (2019)
"If you can, change this system" -Pregnant asylum seekers' perceptions on social determinants and material circumstances affecting their health whilst living in state-provided accommodation in Germany - a prospective, qualitative case study Found at https://bmcpublichealth.biomedcentral.com/articles/10.1186/s12889-019-6481-2

Wadsworth, Y. (1998). 'What is participatory action research?' [online]. Action Research International, Paper 2. www.scu.edu.au/schools/gcm/ar/ari/p-ywadsworth98.html

Institute for community studies found at https://icstudies.org.uk

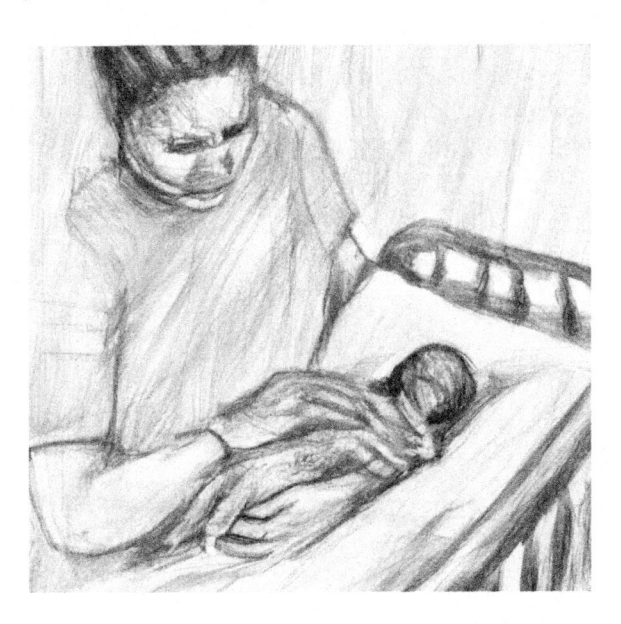

What is it like to live in a refuge as an asylum seeker and be a new mum?

Abstract

Living in a refuge for new mothers is a fantastic way to keep vulnerable parents and babies together. These conditions posed a significant risk of violating the children's human rights, including the right to survival, safety and development; an adequate standard of living; the best possible health; family life, and the right to play.(https://www.cypcs.org.uk/news-and-stories/asylum-seeking-mums-and-babies-finally-moved-to-more-suitable-housing/)

This study shows there are joys and downfalls to living in a refuge.

By Sattia, Aminata, Mariam, and Masoomeh

Introduction

We wanted to research this because we are completing a course for citizen social scientists in 2021, and this is an opportunity to try researching with our peers. Because we all live in a refuge, the research about women who are new mothers living there. It was an area that we had expertise in. We could have just asked amongst ourselves, but we wanted to hear about the other women's experiences, so we tried to involve everybody.

Background

SERCO owns this refuge and is a place for up to 20 asylum seekers. Every woman has their own room and shares three kitchens and one lounge.

Women are sent here because they are considered vulnerable because they are pregnant. Many women are split up from their baby's father and do not know the father, so they are alone in their situation. Some have families in other cities split up with the asylum policy of placing all pregnant women together, so they have their visits to families weekly if there was no covid.

Methods

Using a focus group to draw attention to certain areas we can all discuss the real feelings about living in a refuge for asylum seekers. Using a huge flipchart, we can all record our feelings as we talk. It will be more reliable if we get notes as we do the group rather than remembering them later. Each researcher also took notes of who said what so we could put the respondents' numbers to the write up. The study is a qualitative method called ethnography.

Participants

Asking peers what they feel like living as an asylum seeker could cause unsettled feelings especially if they have dark thoughts about people in the refuge. However, this research got us talking and discussing problems. The questions are in the appendix. We asked all the residents if they wanted to come to the lounge with their babies to form a focus group. We did not want to leave people out. Seven women of different ages and nationalities came to sit with us. All the women have lived in the refuge in Coventry from 4 months to 7 months so far so none of the new ladies joined us, but this was probably because the meeting was in English.

Participant	Age	Country of birth and time in the UK
Participant 1 7month old baby	29	Sierra Leone been in UK 1year 2 months.
Participant 2 4 month old baby	23	Nigerian been in the UK 1year 4 months
Participant 3 7 month old baby	36	Iran been here 1 year and 2 months
Participant 4 7 month old baby		Gambia I have been here 1 year and 4 months
Participant 5 5 month old baby	35	South Africa I have been in the UK 1 year
Participant 6	42	Kenya been here 14 years
Participant 7	29	Kenya been in the UK 3 years

This is a convenience sample because we all live together.

Ethical Considerations

Studying as a participant or peer group of other asylum seekers may mean we all say the same things, and no one says positive things, so we must be careful to record their words carefully and not influence them. The posters will help our memory as I write up what they said.

We will allow people not to answer or not to join the focus group, and they have the right to withdraw. The consent form in the appendix shows the ladies that they can withdraw anytime, and we will not gossip about what they say. The meeting for the focus group is confidential. We treated this session as a serious research project.

Analysis of the Focus Group

This was written up on flip charts as the women shared details and later typed up against the different sections. The plan was to work in 3 sections (see appendix 2) In The first session, we read out the consent letter and told everyone they would have their ideas written down, but we would need to identify them in the write-up.

Section 1 in the Beginning

We used the discussion stimulus in Appendix 2 to cover all sorts of areas, like why you came to the UK.

The group shared they had all been in the UK over a year; been in the UK 1year 2 months,1 year 2 months, 1 year 4 months ,1 year 4 months, 3 years, 14 years.

The women have all been asylum seekers for a long time 2 years ,1year 5 months, 1 year 4 months, 1 year 2 months, 11 months, 8 months, and 8 months.

Tell me about your journey to the UK and why did you come to the UK?
To seek protection (participant 1)
To save myself because I was going through a lot(participant 2)
Because I wasn't safe in my country, and I want to save my life in the UK (participant 3)
I came to the UK for the safety of me and my unborn child (participant 5
I came to the UK for the safety of me and my unborn child (participant 4
For security reasons (participant 6)

The women shared stories about the journey to the UK, and many were very planned; I came by plane and landed at Heathrow Airport (participant 6)

I came with a plane; I claimed asylum here (participant 5)

However, some women travelled across many countries. I have a long story about coming to the UK because it is not easy for my country to get to the UK, but I changed my plan 2-3 times. I was on the way one week finally, I arrived here(participant 3)

The asylum seekers came to the UK for various reasons, primarily seeking protection, safety, and security. Some fled female circumcision and arranged marriages. Each participant in the group had unique circumstances and experiences that led them to leave their home countries and seek refuge in the UK. Some faced threats to their lives and well-being, while others sought safety for themselves and their unborn children.

Participant 1 explicitly states that they came to the UK for protection, which is why many seek asylum in a new country. Participant 2 emphasises the urgency of their situation, stating that they came to save themselves as they were going through a lot in their home country.

Participant 3 echoes similar sentiments, highlighting that they were unsafe in their country and sought refuge in the UK to save their lives. Participant 4 also mentions the safety of themselves and their unborn child as the motivating factor for their journey to the UK.

For Participant 5, the safety and protection of themselves and their unborn child were the primary reasons for seeking asylum in the UK. Participant 6 stated, "for security reasons," implying that they faced threats to their safety and well-being in their country of origin.

Some participants shared their journey to the UK, indicating that the process was often challenging and required careful planning. Participant 6 mentions travelling by plane and landing at Heathrow Airport. Participant 5 also arrived by plane and claimed asylum upon arrival.

Participant 3 explains that their journey to the UK was challenging, involving multiple changes in plans and taking approximately one week to arrive in the UK finally.

Overall, asylum seekers came to the UK to escape dangerous and difficult circumstances in their home countries and seek safety, protection, and security. Their stories illustrate their hardships, the risks they took, and their hopes for finding a better and safer life in the UK. These individual narratives show the courage and determination of asylum seekers as they undertake challenging journeys in pursuit of a new beginning and a chance for a secure and stable future.

Section 2 Experiences

The focus of the discussion shifted to asylum-seeking, with participants sharing how long they had been asylum seekers and describing their experiences. Many women mentioned living in Coventry, with a few expressing dissatisfaction due to being forced to live there by the Home Office or risk losing financial support. The living conditions in the refuge were particularly concerning, especially when providing a suitable environment for their babies to play.

During the middle of the focus group, the participants talked about their experiences as mothers in a refuge. They discussed their favourite aspects of being a mother and the challenges they faced. Some shared their experiences of being moved to Coventry while pregnant, leading to losing connection with friends and living in dirty conditions in the refuge.

Results

Participant 1 said.

It's difficult being an asylum seeker, there are many challenges the things I didn't expect are happening. I have been in asylum more than 1 year and it's taking a lot of time. Before I felt bad because it was almost three months to give birth, I moved to Coventry but thanks to God I have friends to talk to. My baby is a beautiful girl; she is so active, adorable and fun to be with, I feel good seeing her despite the challenges I feel good to have her. The joy I am having looking at my baby knowing that she is really mine.

Now I know that I'm a strong woman, I never knew that I could take care of my baby by myself, and now I know I'm a superwoman.

Participant 2 said.

It is stressful and good because you must stay in the country illegally. Living in Coventry is so stressful because where I came from is better than Coventry, I don't enjoy living in Coventry. My baby is a good boy, he's a darling, and he's everything to me. My favourite thing about being a mum is good because looking at my baby and knowing he is mine is a blessing. My experience being a mum here is so amazing, and I'm so happy I have a boy; the bad thing is being alone and caring for him.

Participant 3 said.

As an asylum seeker, I didn't have any experience before, but it was difficult and stressful because I didn't know about this process and how long I had to wait. Before, I was not in Coventry when I arrived in the UK because I didn't know about my pregnancy; I felt so bad being sent to live in Coventry. My baby is everything to me. I thank God for giving me this miracle in my life. It was my new experience. I was so excited really, it's so difficult because it changes your life behaviour and everything. Experience of being a mom is good, but living here is not easy it makes me sad

Participant 4 said.

Being an asylum seeker is not easy because you don't know what you are going to be going through, but I am glad I went through it. Living in Coventry wasn't easy because I don't know anyone here and it is so stressful in this refuge. I thank God for having such a cute and adorable baby. Favourite thing is I enjoy being a mom because before I had a child too and I love kids. Experience is it was so difficult being a mom is not easy because they are somethings you have to take care of for the baby. My challenges about living here were good because I have experienced a lot of things with the baby. The experience is very good for me because I'm experiencing a lot of culture I do not know, I enjoyed living with people from different culture. I'm coping with it because I'm experiencing a lot with being alone with my baby so it's good for me.

Participant 5 said

It's hard, whoever knows you are an asylum seeker treats you as nothing. You need to ask for help all the time, you need to wait and don't know how long you need to get your papers. It's nice, nicest place I've lived since I got here because of the support I get from charities and refugees so it's nice. My baby is a boy 9-month-old, born in Nottingham city hospital. My favourite thing about being a mom is the responsibility of caring for someone, the feeling of knowing you brought life to the world. I like being a mom. The good thing about being a mom while seeking refuge is that you don't lack for the kids; the charities and organisations support you. The bad thing about being a mom while seeking refuge is that sometimes you need help with the baby, it's not help money can buy. My challenges with being a mom while seeking refuge are that sometimes I need help to afford things I would like for me and my son, being in shared accommodation, not having enough space, and sleeping on a single bed. Baby needs space to play its quite challenging living conditions are not good for mom and baby; this place is not meant for mother and baby.

Participant 6 said.

It's difficult because you must rely on the charities and Home Office and can't provide for yourself. I love Coventry, friendly, helpful and it's a nice place. My baby is 5 months old; he is a baby everything is good about him. It's caring for my baby and all the things that come with caring for a baby. Being a new mom, I didn't know most things, but I got to a lot of help from the moms here and the professionals, the midwives.

Participant 7 said.

Amazingly, everyone is here to help you; different charities are here to help you. My baby is 6 months old, he's a lovely little boy. My favourite thing is its amazing being a mom, it makes you very active. The fact that you see different baby and knowing you can do it. The good thing is taking care of the kid and seeing different moms. The bad thing is the environment is not conducive for the babies to play and no one to help you.

In conclusion, the participants in the discussion expressed a mixture of positive and negative experiences related to motherhood and seeking asylum. They appreciated the support they received from various charities, highlighting the positive aspect of having assistance during challenging times. The joy of being a mother and witnessing the growth and development of their babies was evident in their responses, with one participant describing her 6-month-old son as a lovely little boy.

Being a mother brought a sense of fulfilment and increased activity for some participants, emphasising the positive impact of motherhood on their lives. Additionally, interacting with other mothers and their babies brought a sense of camaraderie and mutual understanding.

However, the participants also mentioned the challenges they faced in the refugee environment. The lack of play areas for babies was a significant concern, highlighting the need for improved living conditions to support their children's development and well-being. Additionally, some participants felt the absence of a robust support system, noting that having someone to help them would have been beneficial.

Overall, the discussion revealed the resilience of these mothers in the face of difficult circumstances. Despite the challenges, they found joy and fulfilment in motherhood and appreciated the support they received from charitable organisations. Addressing the concerns related to living conditions and access to support systems would be crucial in ensuring a more positive experience for asylum-seeking mothers and their babies.

Section 3 challenges.

Then the discussion turned to any challenges and anything they needed help with. The charities providing clothes and food were discussed at length, and the respondents all agreed they would need help to be much better off. They did say the clothes and food caused arguments about sharing, though and this caused stress. They wished they had their pack of food with their own name on it. Many women did not appreciate being housed with so many other mothers. Shared accommodation cause problems since 20 women live here. The differences between women are often worse because they share a tiny house, bathroom and kitchen.

Participant 1 said on the flipchart titled

"The good and bad things about living in the refuge"

A lot of bad things; let's say I'm living her life each time she calls, I have to respond. Three ladies mentioned bullying. My challenges are living with different kinds of people with multiple cultures; people don't respect other's views, and they look down on people. It made me realise that in every situation, you have to cope; now I have realised that I don't need to waste my anger it has helped me to control my anger; I look at things and ignore them.

Participant 2 said

It's not easy being here alone while being an asylum seeker with the baby alone without any help, but I am glad I met some good people I talk with to pass the time. Experiences being in a shared accommodation with multiple cultures is so challenging because you get to know different people. Coping without any help is not easy because it's my first time, and I did it, so I thank God we are doing fine.

Participant 3 said

When you are a new mom, it's not so easy because I don't know how I can take care of my baby; when she cries, I don't know what to do but it is a nice challenge. When I came here seven months ago, everything was new for me, but now we have a lot of problems multiple cultures is good you learn a lot but sometimes it makes me angry you don't have privacy. Just God is helping me to cope with my life without any help.

Participant 4 said

Experience is it was so difficult being a mom is not easy because there are some things you must take care of for the baby. My challenges with living here were good because I have experienced a lot of things with the baby. The experience was very good for me because I'm experiencing a lot of cultures I do not know; I enjoyed living with people from different cultures. I'm coping with it because I'm experiencing a lot of being alone with my baby, so it's good for me.

Participant 5 said

My challenges about being a mom while seeking refuge is that sometimes I'm not able to afford things I would like for myself and my son, being in a shared accommodation not having enough space, and sleeping on a single bed. Baby needs space to play its quite challenging living conditions are not good for mom and baby; this place is not meant for mother and baby.

It's bad!!! And one good is to live with multiple cultures. Meanwhile, you get to learn other people's cultures. There are people to talk to; you are not alone. Everything else is bad, from the kitchen to the bathroom; we fight for food and clothes and so many things; some use us to get what they want, but we are one that's the nicest thing.

As I said, when you live with people at some point, others become friends and family you are not alone, there are people you can talk to take away stress, but it's hard; we force ourselves to cope.

Participant 7 said

My challenges are being here not knowing when your case will be heard and not knowing you are going to be in your own place It's quite nice sometimes, it's a bit hard being alone in such a place that is not conducive. It's hard you need help; you can't do things no one can look after your baby its ab bit difficult.

The challenges faced by the asylum-seeking mothers living in the refuge were evident throughout the discussion. Several key difficulties emerged, pointing to the harsh realities of shared accommodation, limited resources, and the emotional toll of being away from their home countries.

Living in Shared Accommodation: The women expressed their struggles with sharing living spaces with many other asylum-seeking mothers, which led to disagreements, stress, and a lack of privacy. Sharing a tiny house, bathroom, and kitchen with multiple cultures resulted in tensions and differences among the residents.

Lack of Support: Many participants highlighted inadequate support, especially for new mothers with newborns. They were coping without any help, and lacking guidance on childcare added to the challenges they faced.

Financial Constraints: Participants mentioned financial difficulties, making it hard to afford essential items for themselves and their babies. The limited space in the shared accommodation also made it challenging to provide a suitable environment for their children to play and thrive.

Uncertain Future: The uncertainty surrounding their asylum cases and needing to know when they will have their place added to the stress and difficulties they encountered.

Despite these challenges, the women also found some positive aspects of living in the refuge, such as learning about different cultures and forming connections with other asylum seekers. The support and companionship they found among one another helped ease the burden of their circumstances.

The data portrays a complex and challenging experience for asylum-seeking mothers in the refuge. They face hardships related to living conditions, lack of support, and uncertain futures. Their stories underscore the importance of providing adequate resources and support to asylum seekers, especially mothers with young children, as they navigate their journey to a better life in a new country. Addressing these challenges and providing a more supportive environment could significantly contribute to asylum-seeking mothers' and their babies' well-being and resilience.

Discussion of the Findings

All the group said they enjoyed being a mum, but there were challenges where they lived and in the UK policy of not responding to asylum seekers' claims.

The UK government says they will respond quickly to asylum seekers "quote" yet many women are waiting for years and years to get through the system.

All the women came to the UK for safety and security in their life. They fear being sent back. They feel they are treated as a lower class because they are asylum seekers.

The people in the focus group were glad they were now mums and even enjoyed coping all alone sometimes "like superwoman".

The conditions in the refuge are challenging with some in the focus group saying they are fed up with the electricity cutting out all the time. They are also fed up if others do not clean the bathroom after them.

The accommodation could be better and the focus group discussed the kitchens with tiny little fridges for everyone and the bedrooms with dampness and poor furniture.

They were glad they had accommodation since many asylum seekers are homeless and destitute.

"It is shocking to see how women who have already survived extreme violence and abuse are being left with no support when they come to the UK to seek safety. These punitive policies leave women who have already gone through rape and torture vulnerable to abuse in this country. Too often, our government ignores the needs of women who cross borders. It is time to build a fairer asylum process in which women are protected from harm and can be supported to live with dignity." (https://www.refugeewomen.co.uk/not-safe/)

References

Women for Refugee Women and regional partners publish their new report, Will I ever be safe? Asylum-seeking women made destitute in the UK.

IN THEIR OWN WORDS

Asylum seekers moms experiences of feeding (introducing solid foods) their babies in a sharing accommodation Coventry UK in 2021 by Emira

Abstract

This work results from the Coventry Citizen Science course Coventry University ran in April 2021. I was taking part in the course; this is my first research. English is my second language, and I speak Albanian. I just gave birth to my beautiful son, Arbor, in Sept 2020. I am now trying to wean him and ensure he gets the best nutrients and food while living on very little money and sleeping in a refuge for asylum seekers.

Introduction

Weaning your baby is a process that takes patience and understanding from both babies and moms. In sharing accommodation this beautiful process becomes difficult for various reasons. Preparing baby food at home is the best thing you can do as it is even healthier for babies also less expensive but the lack of refrigerators to store baby food is one of the main problems for mothers in this house.

Preparing every meal for the baby is tiring because the baby wants a lot of care and time so in that time when we are free choose to cook and so can store the food for other days or meals during the day. The charity Carriers of Hope has supplied a large chest freezer for baby food but until now moms have been unable to do so.

Another thing that makes difficult this process are kitchen basics you will probably find that you already don't have most of the equipment needed to make home-cooked meals for your baby there are certain pieces of equipment ,store cupboard essentials sterilising equipment processors and blenders(electric food processors or blenders make it easy to purée large quantities of food quickly).Steaming vegetables preserves maximum nutrients so it's well worth having a steamer but in this condition we try to find alternatives .

Methods

Peer research is a participatory research method in which people with lived experience of the issues being studied take part in directing and conducting the research. Like other participatory methods, peer research 'recognises that individuals within any community being researched are themselves competent agents, capable of participating in research on a variety of levels, including as researchers. It aims to move away from the 'extractive' model of social research and to empower people to affect positive change by participating in research on their own communities.

This work is the result of asking women in the refuge where I live about their experiences of feeding their baby.

The research method is a case study of a refuge with 20 asylum-seeking women who have just been moms this year.

So this research is about how they find feeding their babies difficult/easy preparing their food and whether the money is enough for them. Are they experiencing of feeding like they have imagined before?

Research methods refers to the tools that one uses to do research. These can either be qualitative or quantitative or mixed. Quantitative methods examine numerical data and often requires the use of statistical tools to analyse data collected. More precisely, research methods help us get a solution to a problem. ... The study of research methods gives training to apply them to a problem. The study of research methodology provides us the necessary training in choosing methods, materials, scientific tools and training in techniques relevant for the problem chosen. The women participants speak different languages and have different cultures, so my methodology included speaking to them and sending them a very short questionnaire on google forms. See appendix 1.

This is such small research that uses mixed methods; it is qualitative and quantitive.

When collecting and analysing data, quantitative research deals with numbers and statistics, while qualitative research deals with words and meanings. Both are important for gaining different kinds of knowledge.

I sent out a questionnaire to all the ladies in the refuge. Some won't answer because it is in English, but I can observe them with their babies in the kitchen and do a semi-structured interview there. Often, they can speak more English than they read.

Quantitative research is expressed in numbers, and the questionnaire app makes the data into graphs. Participant observation is a qualitative research method in which the researcher not only observes the research participants but also actively engages in the activities of the research participants. Most researchers who conduct participant observations take on the role they are interested in studying.

Common quantitative methods include experiments, observations recorded as numbers, and surveys with
Qualitative research is expressed in words. It is used to understand concepts, thoughts, or experiences. This type of research enables you to gather in-depth insights on topics that must be better understood.

Common qualitative methods include interviews with open-ended questions, observations described in words, and literature reviews that explore concepts and theories.

So for this study, I will ask semi-structured questions in an interview-style about the mummies experiences of feeding and preparing their baby's food

This Survey will make it possible to understand the experience of every mother who lives in this accommodation and is going through a difficult period in their life as they are awaiting a response from the interior ministry. All these that I mentioned above affect this process so beautiful but also quite difficult due to different circumstances. This will make it possible to identify these essential problems for any new mother who is not properly prepared. Those interviews will be good finding the information.

Ethical Considerations

One of the main principles of research is that participation should be voluntary no one is obliged to participate in my survey. Because we share the same house, it will be easier for me to communicate with them but also this can also become a problem as they may share some information more than they should, and this makes me responsible to act or not.

If I see any danger to myself or the person I am interviewing, I will be forced to talk to people competent for such issues.

Literature

Key elements in achieving good nutrition are ensuring the accessibility and availability of affordable healthy food.
Choice preference, familiarity and the social context of food are also cited by Manandhar (2005) as desirable for healthy eating. The 2005 research with ten asylum seekers identified problems: the previous home diets were much healthier, with lots more fruit and vegetables than when they became asylum seekers. They could not eat on demand and tended to use processed food given by charities, which affected their ability to breastfeed. The asylum seekers money goes on more expensive ethnic food (Henjum et al 2019). The ability to get a bus to better, cheaper shops is affected by a need for more money for bus fares. Children's needs and debt avoidance are prioritised over food spending. (Manandhar 2005)

Childcare language cultural differences and mental health problems are all identified in the research as factors that stop good healthy food for asylum seekers and their baby.

IN THEIR OWN WORDS

Asylum seekers moms' experiences of feeding (introducing solid foods) their babies in a sharing accommodation in Coventry, UK in 2021

Weaning your baby is a process that takes patience and understanding from both babies and moms. In sharing accommodation this beautiful process becomes difficult for various reasons. Why is it difficult?

What helps you when you are weaning your baby? The group all started weaning about 6 months and this was because the babies seemed to be hungrier needing more than formula or breast.

The mummies all said they enjoyed it when their baby took their first food. Some were worried they could choke their baby. Carriers of Hope, a charity, had shown the food the baby could have once they were sitting up, but it was still worrying.

The mummies said

"exciting to see him eat food for the first time."

"I started by giving him fruits. Blended papaya."

The charities bring lots of baby food in jars but not many mummies use them *"I chose to make fresh food for my baby because I am sure there's no preservatives and it is made hygienically."*

The barriers to making good food for their baby were all the same.

A few women mentioned the problem of hygiene and space to prepare food. *There are few work surfaces in the kitchen, and they are always full.*

Cleaning clothes and liquids cost lots of money from the shops, so the babies make a mess with their food, and it is a problem. Many need more money to buy blenders and mashers to make the adults' food into baby food.

"I do have the basic equipment to prepare and cook my baby's food. It's a shared kitchen so the condition is not very good, but I clean the worktop before preparing the baby food."

A big barrier is buying food for baby and as they get older, they need more variety and nutritious food. Some feed their baby-on-baby rice all the time. Others cook new things but there is a lot of waste if you cannot freeze the food.

"I shop at Sainsbury's because it's the nearest supermarket or go to the market 20 minutes away by bus. I don't find everything in Sainsbury's that's why I go to the market, especially for African food."

All the mummies are struggling for money to buy food. The tins and pasta from the food banks are only sometimes good for babies weaning because they should not have sugar or salt. Everyone in the group feeds on cheap food but wants the best for their baby.

"My budget is not enough for both of us so I try and get the cheapest for myself"

The mummies often share food with other babies, but some are cross about this because they have money for their baby and think it's unfair -everyone should buy their own. *"If times were better everyone would share and offer food. This makes us feel bad"* Ideas about cheaper food are shared, and the charity worker, Lin, brings us vegetables for the babies weaning.

Summary

This work asks asylum-seeking women who live in a refuge about their feeding and preparing food for their babies.

To write about the experiences of asylum-seeking mothers in the first place, you must be one of them yourself. At first glance, you may think it is very simple for them as they have everything paid for them. Or mothers have enough time to prepare food for their little ones. But no, the issue is deeper than it seems at first glance after living without having any motive for your future, to be stressed or even depressed adding to it and the lack of basic appliances in the kitchen make you feel very bad emotionally.

The research takes time to dedicate time to and on my part to be a young single mother taking care of my baby. That these times have been a little difficult period for me too. It is difficult, and I did this work only at night after the baby fell asleep.

From this work, I have noticed that living in an accommodation where you must share with 20 other women and prepare baby food correctly is difficult. The reasons are different, but the main ones are these: Lack of equipment basic in the kitchen such as a steamer food processor or blender. Not living close to convenient and cheaper shops to buy the food you need and at more reasonable prices for us as asylum seekers. Not having the right information about what foods to give and what to avoid monthly. Having children allergic to milk protein and on the other hand you do not have a dietitian to recommend what the baby should consume. The stress and anxiety that everyone experiences for personal reasons turn this very beautiful experience into an experience with great difficulty.

Recommendations

Access to food

Do not put refugees outside the city away from the shops -put them in a community with shops.

Increase the allowances for asylum seekers.

Have someone in the services responsible for food poverty for children.

Speed up the application process so we can live in a community, not a refuge and we can work.

Get charities to bring a variety of affordable cultural food or tell us how to buy them. Put on a bus to get us to the cheaper shops once a week.

Give more teaching about food

Breast feeding and pregnant women should be given fresh food and support for mental health.

Nutrition and cooking projects like the one from Carriers of Hope should be everywhere.

Getting the moms to cook and freeze ethnic food will develop an understanding of baby feeding.

Give nutritional courses to new mums.

Food is important in everyday life, but my research shows it is very important to asylum seekers who have very little choice but food banks and expensive shops next to the refuge.

Appendix 1 interview questions

Asylum seekers moms' experiences of feeding (introducing solid foods) their babies in a sharing accommodation in Coventry UK in 2021

Weaning your baby is a process that takes patience and understanding from both babies and moms. In sharing accommodation this beautiful process becomes difficult for various reasons. Why is it difficult?

What helps you when you are weaning your baby?

How do you learn about weaning?

References

MDPI and ACS Style

Henjum, S.; Caswell, B.L.; Terragni, L. "I Feel like I'm Eating Rice 24 Hours a Day, 7 Days a Week": Dietary Diversity among Asylum Seekers Living in Norway. Nutrients 2019, 11, 2293. https://doi.org/10.3390/nu11102293

Manandhar , M (2005) Food, Nutrition and Poverty Among Asylum-Seekers in North-West Ireland

Psychological Toll and Educational Challenges Faced by Teenagers in the Asylum Process: A Case Study by Gloria

Abstract

This research delves into the often-overlooked psychological impact experienced by teenagers who undergo the asylum process alongside their parents. The study sheds light on the persistent mental torture these young individuals endured even after gaining asylum. Additionally, it examines the adverse effects on their mental health, evidenced by various challenges faced during their educational journey. The research further explores the dual battles parents fought, navigating their asylum cases and advocating for their children's mental well-being and educational opportunities. Through in-depth case studies and qualitative analysis, this research highlights the urgent need for comprehensive support systems for asylum-seeking families and calls for measures to protect affected teenagers' psychological well-being and educational prospects.

Most teenagers who go through the asylum process with their parents go through some form of mental torture that persists even after they get their status. Many teenagers in the asylum process with their parents are having issues with their mental health. For example, this study evidences several teenagers who have gone to school with their peers. At the end of their education, they happen to be refused a place in their choice of study all because their status does not allow them access to Further education or higher education.

Most parents I work with as a volunteer are fighting double battles in that, as they fight for their asylum cases, they are also fighting for their children's mental well-being and educational opportunities. This work is a case study of 5 teenagers and their views on their educational opportunities.

Background

I have chosen this topic to research because of the ordeals I know the young people are going through in terms of education just because they are asylum seekers. Being aware of a few cases in my community, I decided to research to find out more to bring the situation to the awareness of other people. Those who read it will understand how teenagers can get behind in their work or feel education could be more useful. Many people need to come on board to find some solutions, but the power is with the educational policy in the UK. Many teenagers are journeying with their parents and siblings to settle in this country. I strongly believe that there is a problem, and this is affecting the young adults in our communities.

"In the UK, people seeking refugee protection can't access higher education. Although they've come here legally, fleeing persecution to claim asylum under international law, the UK classes asylum seekers as international students. They are charged international fees, unable to access student loans and unable to work, meaning that higher education, a right for all under the Universal Declaration of Human Rights (article 26), is out of reach". (https://www.ucas.com/connect/blogs/uk-university-scholarships-refugees-and-asylum-seekers-open-applications)

Aims

This research aims to identify young asylum seekers' barriers at school.

To find out what they say supports them in education and to write some recommendations for education and charities and parents to help young people to make the most of their educational opportunities.

Methods

This is a qualitative method of gathering data. Qualitative research approach is an approach used to understand people's attitudes, behaviours, opinions, and many more to achieve generalised results from a sample population.

I am using a semi-structured interview which has its advantages and disadvantages. A semi-structured interview is a method which provides a clear set of questions or instructions for interviewers, and this can give reliable, comparable qualitative data.

An advantage of a semi-structured interview is that it encourages two-way communication in which both candidate and the interviewer are allowed to ask questions that allows for a comprehensive discussion of the relevant topic. This method can help me get tangible information from the individuals I have in mind to interview.

Its disadvantage is that sitting down with interviewers takes time to conduct an open-ended interview.

As a researcher, it is important to understand the research methods to be used because the design dictates the data collected, and it needs to answer the question set by the researcher.

I used the survey method with those of my participants, who have no access to the internet and therefore cannot join a Zoom interview with me. Some of my participants preferred speaking to me outside their homes because they still live with their parents and would not like to bring back painful memories that would tear their parents and siblings apart.

Ethics

Research ethics are important because it helps you to plan the entire research before starting. It is very important to protect and safeguard the research information of the participants during the research, as the data collected is confidential. The fact that participants are all from different backgrounds might have different understandings and therefore needs to be taken care of and protected because some of the information might be crucial and confidential to that person. Other people should not know what the participant answered. The information must be kept confidential, an important part of the research process. There are so many confidentiality factors where information is concerned, such as maintaining trust, because of the volatility of most of the participants involved. Participants should be informed about how data will be collected, used, analysed, stored, and featured in a report.

In my research, young people are answering the questions, so ethics with them should be more than ethics with adults who may have more worldly experience. Extra caution to be confidential and not tell their mates. Extra vigilance to safeguard them if they tell me they use a gang to fit into society or carry a knife. I am still determining what I will find, but I will use supervision from my volunteering role to ensure I follow safeguarding rules. My research involves vulnerable young people and their parents who have been through trauma. Unhealthy relationships or multiple traumas have occurred to these respondents in their life already. The research must be carried out sensitively and with an understanding of the sense of exploitation -which will bring adverse effects on individuals and will be unhealthy.

I should think carefully before entering multiple relationships with any individual or group, such as participants in my research studies. I must not use my position as a researcher to engage participants in any other additional research duties that are not required of me. I owe it to my participants to outline my duty and structure of the research relationship before I begin with them. Individual rights need to be prioritised, and so for those of my participants who requested to have their interviews outside their homes, I had to let it be as they wished.

Those who prefer to be interviewed whilst their parents are in, I allowed them. I also interviewed participants in the park because that was their preference.

Even though I knew some of the participants, I did not encourage any form of irresponsible behaviour towards participants during our interviews. Before starting, I asked for participants' consent and assured them their information would be protected and kept safe. Participants are being made aware that I will let them know the outcome at the end of the research. I also assured participants that I would not use or mention their names to anyone.

My ethical sheet to sign is in Appendix 1, and the questions I asked are in Appendix 2

Literature review

My work is about the ordeals of asylum-seeking children and their parents during the asylum process. This was narrowed down to only the teenagers in the asylum process. Many teenagers seek asylum with their parents, leaving many mentally paralysed, depressed, anxious, and reserved among their peers. Montgomery, (2011).

I noticed this in my community, but I will read more literature to check that this is not just a local issue for teens. Many have thought of self-harm and admitting that they are nothing on the face of the earth because they believe *"the Home Office wants them to look that way"* (respondent 3).

I chose this topic because I have lived the experience of being an asylum seeker with a child who is not yet a teenager, but the type of questions my child asks shows how the asylum process affects children. If children who cannot express themselves well could notice that something is not right about their state, how much more do teenagers feel concerned?

When I have conversations with the parents of those teenagers, I realise that if something is not done to resolve the reasons why teenagers are getting depressed, we may end up losing our sanity as well as our children. It is very difficult to parent teenagers at times, but these families have extra care for their young people.

'All children have the right to education, which is enshrined in the UN Convention on the Rights of the Child'(UNICEF.org.uk). Still, many research papers identify that despite this right, children continue to face obstacles when being educated as asylum seekers or refugees in the UK.

Results Research Findings

A lack of support is identified when young people think about going to college, which is about poor support leading to poor mental health and discrimination against asylum seekers. Their thoughts are about the world and systems being against them. This takes up a lot of thought and interferes with the teen's schoolwork.

Poor mental health: Out of the 5 participants I interviewed, three acknowledged their mental health was getting bad each time they realised they couldn't further their education because of their status. They felt what was the point in going to school when they would be without a job anyway. Their parents cannot work here. Some teenagers said they were much better at schoolwork than others in the class but would not get a chance to apply for college or university.

Five of them agreed that they were always treated differently in school and college because they are Asylum seekers' children, which affects their performances in class even though they could do well, affecting them mentally.

Participants knew their families had to get papers to remain and work in the UK. One said, *"Why is everything turning against us just because of a paper? Is our mental health not more important than status?"*.

Another participant felt persecuted due to their status and said, *"Now look at the whole time I have wasted learning day and night, only to finish and sit down at home gazing at the ceiling, thinking why am I being killed slowly just because I am an asylum seeker?"*

All the teens admitted to thinking and feeling "inside "themselves in class. *"I cannot even think straight again; these people want to finish me"*. They independently mentioned; *"thinking and thinking"* and going over their future opportunities.

One participant said, *"I am no more myself that is why I see a psychologist every week. I have no interest in anything again".*

Almost all of the participants said the asylum journey is meant to waste their talents and their future, and it is disturbing them mentally. *"We are four siblings, and my Mum has gone through so much just to see us become somebody in future, and now I will never be somebody."*

One teen said, *"They want us to get mad!"* relating to the policy and legislation as if it were a personal attack.

The young people report to the Home Office once a week and then once every two weeks, disrupting their school day. It also gives the impression to others in their class that they are different; they need to be kept an eye on. All respondents said they felt shamed by having to present as an asylum seeker.

Poverty was an issue for all the teens, and they talked about cheap second-hand clothes and shoes that fell apart before the end of the first term. The extra curriculum activities cannot be done due to a lack of kit or a need to babysit other children whilst their mum works.

The asylum seekers with no right to remain are not allowed to work, which adds to the teen's concept of worth for the family. The lack of a computer and pens for school was also an issue for the teens, making them different from their classmates.

Also, the worry about their mums was a big issue. Every problem the mum had they worried about. *"My Mum was once sent bills from the hospital for our treatments, but she was asked not to work."* The unjust and unfair system was a major point in the interviews. They spoke of getting charity food or going hungry at times.

"How can our parents look after us when they are not working?"

Personal poverty meant the teens never had people come to their homes and never met online like others. There was no personal money for any of the teens in my sample, which affected how they saw themselves as big brothers and sisters. *"I cannot even buy anything I want for myself, let alone my siblings."* There was also an aspect of children as carers *"Because it's just my mum, I must do a lot more for my brother."*

There is a definite difference between the teens and others in their peer group in terms of buying power. Often they have to watch others buy sweets. *"My peers laugh at me when we go to the shop to buy."*. Although they live in an inner-city postcode known for poverty, these young people feel even poorer than the other youngsters in the school. The students I interviewed were from Africa, the Gambia, and South Africa, so they had some English language to start school with. They did mention other youngsters who had no chance as they could not speak English. However, they also realised they needed proper English lessons to help them to write as well as they could. This was a drawback in not having a good basis of English language to apply to their schooling.

The last bit of the interviews talked about their aspirations and future. All my participants couldn't go to the university even if they did well because of their status and inability to pay the tuition fees. The teens felt the lack of equality between them and others in their class. They all said they wanted a better education and applied for college or university but felt they cannot.

The interview was rounded up by giving the young people some contacts for organisations that will help refugees and asylum seekers find funding for university https://www.ucas.com/finance/additional-funding/student-finance-refugees-and-asylum-seekers

Conclusions and Recommendations

Schools should	*Voluntary and charity workers should*
1. Plan for asylum seekers and refugee teens to have a dedicated spot for them to meet. 2. Support them with applications for colleges and higher education. 3. Provide pastoral and mental health support 4. Liaison between school and home 5. Ensure that schools have access to good-quality interpreting services! 6. Teach English when needed.	1. Inspire, encourage, and guide the young people to believe in themselves. 2. Take extra training about the barriers for young people. 3. Continue activities that create friendships in the community. 4. Continue to supply uniforms (Carriers of Hope)

References

Montgomery, E., 2011. Trauma, exile and mental health in young refugees. Acta Psychiatrica Scandinavica, 124, pp.1-46.

Transitioning through education for refugee and asylum-seeking young people in the UK found at https://www.unicef.org.uk/policy/education-transitions-refugees-report/ 3/3/2021

UNHCR (2019) Stepping Up: Refugee education in crisis (UNHCR);

Appendix 1 Consent Forms

As a researcher, the consent forms should be clear about the reasons or aims of my research. I must make them aware for the fact that, the research is without any pay or rewards and for that matter, they have a choice. I also must make it clear that if they tell me anything that will hurt them or others, I will have a duty to tell; for example if they self-harm or are being bullied, I would have to act.

Hello, my name is Gloria, and I am doing research about The state of teenagers during the Asylum process.

Participants must be aware of how information will be collected, so I will ask you a few questions about your school life, and I will make notes as you tell me. The notes will be private and not shared. You can refuse to answer any of my questions; if you get bored, you can withdraw your answers. It will take about 20 minutes.

Ultimately, I will tell your story to other researchers, but they will not need to learn your identity. This is important because we need to hear the young people's views on what it is like for them.

Appendix 2 The Questions

How old are you?
What is your Country of Origin?
How do you feel about finishing school and applying for college?
Do you know that and need help to go further to university?
Can you tell me something about being an Asylum seeker journey with your family?
If you can now go and further your education, how would you feel?

Asylum Seekers' Welfare and Support System: Unraveling the Realities and Perceptions in Coventry
by Dr Lin Armstrong

Introduction

Alongside many in the host country, I believe the women who are asylum seekers have services and money given to them, so they are as ok as any of us in Coventry. As I researched for this work, I found many facts that supported this view.

Asylum support is from the 1999 Immigration Act. Exception 95 gives people money on a green card like a debit card with limitations. Asylum support is only for people with their first asylum claim or those who have had a baby whilst claiming. Everyone else is classed as section 4; women whose claims have been rejected or who are making subsequent requests. Section 4 women have the same Aspen card but cannot be used at a cash point. Asylum seekers can use it to buy in a shop or top up mobiles.

The women get £36 -£40 a week for toiletries and clothing, prams etc., accommodation and all bills at the refuge are paid for.

The notion that the asylum seekers are not in absolute poverty is supported by the fact that they can claim a maternity grant; £350 as a one-off for baby clothes, cots and bedding. There is a difference across the country; sometimes, they get a second maternity grant. The woman can only apply 6-8 weeks before the birth and need an original certificate Mat B1 to get a maternity grant.(https://www.gov.uk/asylum-support/what-youll-get)

Therefore, from the outside, the policy covering asylum seekers seems beneficial and fair.

Background

Many vulnerable migrant groups, such as refused asylum seekers, trafficked people, undocumented migrants, pregnant women and children are more susceptible to ill health and mortality than other vulnerable groups and their UK-born counterparts. (International Organisation of Migration. Maternal and Child Healthcare for Immigrant Populations [Internet]. Brussels; 2009.)

Pregnant women seeking asylum are identified as a vulnerable group with specific health and well-being problems and concerns, according to Aspinall and Watters (2010).

Many studies carried out between 2000-2010 highlighted that asylum seekers had poor experiences in the U.K., and the cause was that the professionals were not meeting their health and social care needs. Gaudion and Allotey (2008) listed the key findings of their study as entitlement and access issues may not necessarily be well understood by asylum-seeking communities, resulting in late or non-presentation to maternity services. They also reported a reliance on others to communicate the women's lifestyle through translators. Communication problems led to women believing they were going to die during childbirth. Due to an over-reliance on family and friends, multilingual members of the community, a lot of information was missed out or not disclosed.

Waugh (2010), researching asylum seekers in Leeds, UK, found they were often isolated, homeless, and impoverished. They received various standards of community care from midwives and often could not get interpreters. In total, 24 births were discussed in Waugh's study, where most women originated from African countries, with the remainder from China, Iraq, Syria and Palestine.

Shortall et al. (2013-2017) did a longitudinal study of 35 asylum seekers in a London UK clinic. They found evidence that entitlement checks and filling in forms deterred women from gaining what they were entitled to. The charging for services in a population with little access to primary care also led to the non-take-up of maternity care. Antenatal care is frequently received late and often does not meet the minimum standards for care. It subsequently puts women and their unborn children at increased risk of pregnancy-associated complications. (Shortall et al.)

Coventry has a long history of welcoming refugees and asylum seekers. Still, even here, The Independent (July 2020) reported there are" Vulnerable asylum seekers placed in dozens of hotels across the U.K. since March, where it is claimed they are restricted to set meals and given no support for essentials such as toiletries and baby milk" (Independent newspaper, July 2020) This comment was about asylum seekers who were placed in a hotel for up to a year or more when the outbreak of a pandemic COVID-19, led to even more, delayed the dispersal system.

The participants in this research are well informed of their entitlement and access information from Coventry's well-developed asylum support officer, migrant support, and charity networks. Furthermore, they were not isolated in the community but housed with 20 other new mothers.

Methods

To understand women's experiences, a qualitative interpretive approach was adopted. The semi-structured interview questions followed four stages.

1. Thoughts and feelings when you found out you were pregnant
2. Any thoughts about care throughout the pregnancy
3. The birth and support for your baby now in the refuge
4. Hopes for the future

Once the women's words were noted and often translated, there was a choice to make in how to present the results. The researcher could present each story as a case study in its entirety or theme at the sentence level to make a point. It was felt they could be easily identifiable to their peers if the write-up gave a whole story of age, nationality, and the events they had in their lives. So, in the interests of anonymity, the data was themed at a sentence level and decided using a bottom-up approach. It seems the women wanted to discuss midwives and charities who had helped them, living in the refuge and their fears and hopes for the future.

The reader can see robust qualitative data as themes could be moving around, hospital experiences, breastfeeding, multi-agency work, refuge living and hopes for the future. The data loses nothing from theming but protects the respondents much more. The deliberate tactic of leaving the English as it was in places helps maintain the respondent's" voices. Sometimes a thread could be seen in several headings, so ideas overlapped.

An interview schedule was made up by inviting the women to speak with me online in a Zoom app at specific times. This quickly became shambolic because the women were often interrupted by their baby's needs, and we had to stop and start as convenient. The second-hand computers supplied by the charity Carriers of Hope were sufficient to do" Zoom", but there were only 3 of them, so we made a sharing rota. Later Coventry University supplied a tablet and a dongle to help with the research. The level of expertise needed to use a Zoom call was frustrating for some participants, so we often talked on the phone and in the car park, using interpreters from friendship groups. In this casual way, every 20 women was approached for their story.

Participants

The respondents were recruited from a convenience sample at the refuge I support as a charity worker. The Carriers of Hope are a 'Coventry only' charity, and I started work in the refuge last October -4 months ago using a grant from Children in Need. The women were all allowed to answer my research questions, and two did not because there was no interpreter for their language. Therefore, in this research n=18

Ethical Considerations

The first concern was that the researcher was a charity worker in the refuge, so the women may disclose too much, having built a rapport with the worker. The way around that was to treat the interview as a serious conversation, reading their rights not to take part or withdraw later. The consent must be informed, but this was often difficult due to a lack of shared languages. Therefore, another ethical concern was raised regarding proper informed consent for procedures. This was satisfied by posting the research and consent details onto their "What's app" in different languages.

Messages From Research

Before the baby's birth, the women reported that they had been moved several times, so any links they made were broken to move them to the refuge. It is also of note that throughout the pandemic, the women were moved without testing, making it risky at each stay.

However, many were grateful to get a safe house with other women where they could cook their food which did not happen in hotels.

The beauty of the refuge is that women can cook their food. *In the hotel, they were feeding us at certain times. The chef made lunch, but in the morning, we had cereals and bread, but I needed diabetic food. I am sick when I eat those foods. I have diarrhoea. They were scared it was Covid, and I had the test 3 times. It was the food it wasn't working in my system* (respondent 17)

In Birmingham, the smell of the food in the hotel was not good. The room and the food were not good. I was sick. I was vomiting, so they moved me from Derby. I had no friends there in the new refuge. (respondent 5)

Respondent 3 had three moves in a few months. *I found out I was pregnant in the U.K. I was seven months pregnant, starting life in Derby. I stayed for the birth, and two months later, I was moved. I was in a hotel in Derby, so the Home Office moved me.*

I applied to the Birmingham hotel, so I was told to go to a home that was for pregnant ladies only. I have no family here. (respondent 4).

They moved you even when they moved me, I was two weeks to my due date. (respondent 6)

The home office decided for me to come here from Derby when the baby was two months. I don't have a family. (respondent 8)

I gave birth and moved out with the help of "Migrant Help". They put me in a hotel in Nottingham for three weeks. Then they moved from The Britannia Hotel to this refuge. The hotel was not ok with a small baby. We were in a hotel during the covid pandemic. (respondent 4)

When my child was one month, I needed emergency accommodation in the hotel. Then they moved me here (the refuge) because mother and child can't stay there too long. (respondent 16)

I was moved away from the baby's daddy and my friends in London. I cry every night to go back (respondent 11). *The home office makes me stay here because I have a baby.*

The data provided highlights the frequent moves experienced by asylum seekers during their pregnancy and postpartum period. Respondents 3, 4, 6, 8, 11, and 16 all shared their experiences of being relocated multiple times, often with short notice and little consideration for their specific needs and circumstances.

The frequent moves experienced by these asylum seekers can have significant negative impacts on their physical and mental well-being. Moving to different locations during pregnancy and shortly after childbirth can disrupt access to essential healthcare services, support networks, and community resources. It can also increase stress and anxiety, mainly when the moves are abrupt and unpredictable.

Moreover, being moved to different cities or areas can result in social isolation, as asylum seekers may be separated from friends and family they have made along the way. This lack of stable social support can exacerbate loneliness and vulnerability during a challenging time.

The reasons for these frequent moves are often tied to the decisions made by the Home Office based on their asylum cases and available accommodation options. While the Home Office may have reasons for their choices, it is essential to recognise the potential adverse effects these moves can have on asylum seekers' well-being and mental health, especially pregnant women and new mothers.

Providing stable and secure accommodation, especially during pregnancy and after childbirth, is crucial for the health and safety of asylum seekers. It is essential for the authorities to consider the specific needs and vulnerabilities of pregnant women and new mothers when making relocation decisions and to ensure that their rights and well-being are protected.

Furthermore, addressing asylum seekers' challenges during this period requires a holistic and compassionate approach, considering their unique circumstances and providing appropriate support systems. Such support can go a long way in mitigating frequent moves' negative impacts and promoting asylum seekers' health and resilience during this critical phase of their lives.

Respondents often had a very transient life before giving birth, but some also had big shocks when they tried to join their partners here. The abandonment of the fathers added to their stress.

"I got pregnant in my country three weeks pregnant when I came to the U.K. Nowhere to stay; my partner did not want me here." (respondent 3)

Most of the babies in the refuge were unplanned, *"in the beginning I was in the Gambia. Four weeks later realised I was pregnant- back to Senegal living with my parents"* (respondent 10).

The dad is not in the picture (respondent 6)

I knew I was first pregnant when I missed my period in the U.K. No father for baby. I was visiting with my cousin. My room was small for me and baby I had to move out (respondent 16)

(Respondent 17) *I found out I was pregnant when I got to England and was no longer with my partner. I felt bad. I did not know anybody, but I felt when I had the baby, I would not be alone; he will be everything to me.*

I was hiding in this country, and then when I got pregnant, it meant I had to own up to being here. It endangered my life here. (respondent 18)

In conclusion the data provided highlights the challenging and often tumultuous circumstances pregnant asylum seekers face. These women experienced various hardships, including transient living situations, lack of partner support, unplanned pregnancies, and feelings of isolation. The respondents' narratives shed light on the emotional distress and vulnerability they encountered during this critical phase.

One common theme that emerges is the transient life many of the respondents had before coming to the UK. This instability can profoundly impact their well-being, making it challenging to access consistent healthcare and support services during pregnancy. The lack of stable accommodation and uncertainty about their future compound the stress and anxiety these women face during pregnancy and childbirth.

Another significant concern is fathers' abandonment, leaving many respondents to navigate pregnancy and motherhood alone. This lack of support and involvement from partners can intensify feelings of isolation and vulnerability, making it even more challenging for these women to cope with pregnancy and motherhood's emotional and practical challenges.

Additionally, some respondents disclosed that their pregnancies were unplanned, which can further heighten stress and uncertainty about their future. Being far from home and living in unfamiliar surroundings without the support of loved ones adds to the complexity of their situation.

The fear of being discovered as an asylum seeker while pregnant is also a prevailing concern expressed by one respondent (respondent 18). This fear highlights the precarious position many pregnant asylum seekers find themselves in, as their pregnancy can expose them to potential risks if their immigration status is not secure.

The data underscores the critical need for comprehensive and compassionate support systems for pregnant asylum seekers. Addressing the challenges of transient living, lack of partner support, unplanned pregnancies, and the fear of discovery requires a multifaceted approach. Providing stable and safe accommodation, access to healthcare, mental health support, and community connections can significantly improve the well-being and resilience of pregnant asylum seekers during this vulnerable period in their lives. Additionally, measures to ensure the protection and dignity of these women, regardless of their immigration status, are vital in promoting their overall health and well-being.

Often, they had a dangerous encounter with men, and their life was risky. *"I couldn't get accommodation, so I slept at Victoria train station. A male friend in Coventry put me up. There were two guys living in a shared apartment."* (respondent 3)

It's hard being trafficked. (respondent 4)

Even the selected accommodation was not safe; *I was in the hotel with the baby, then this refuge. There was an incident in the hotel- guys knocking the door and asking for sex. I reported to the social worker, and I had to leave there* (respondent 4).

Often the women had friends and family to put them up, but when they became pregnant, they were asked to leave (respondent 2,11 and 1,17). *I was living with my cousin, and we agreed I would leave soon.*

I was with a friend, but she couldn't keep me when I had a baby. I moved from staying with my friend to the hotel. The home office made me move. I could not eat the food, so I stopped lactating and forced the baby to take the breast. (respondent 17)

Many women quickly become pregnant again, indicating a need for help in family planning and guidance. For some women, their baby was a burden at first, but they could enjoy them with support. The women's refuge seems like a safer, better place than the hotels. They can buy cultural food when living in a refuge but are sick of hotel food. A strong theme in the research is being let down and disappointed in their lives so far.

Most women here have been in the hotel or a hostel before arriving, and all the babies are under one year old. Usually, they will be moved without notice once the baby is one. The women have no security of knowing they can stay here. They will be moving again.

Hospital Experiences

Most of the issues raised by participants in this study have been introduced previously. They are reflected in other recent reviews and enquiries through the Confidential Enquiry into Maternal and Child Health (2007) which identifies poorer outcomes for the babies of minority women. *You have one day at the hospital, and then you come home.* (respondent 7, 4 and 8) (respondents reported being in and out of the hospital quickly, even with underweight babies. Respondent 7 was so scared her baby would die because he was so malnourished; Respondent 4 spent the last weeks of her pregnancy worrying that the baby was too small for dates. It seemed the hospital staff who knew about Asylum seekers responded to them well.

The hospital is so lovely. They tried for me better than back home. The midwife was so lovely she knew about asylum brought me clothes for the baby, and they taught me to breastfeed (respondent 17)

Maternity care appointments and, finally birth seemed to be another thing asylum-seeking mothers do alone. Some reported no one spoke their language in the health system, and some said they were the only asylum seeker in the hospital. One woman did find a friend in the hospital.

I was with another girl from Albanian. The midwife helped me with everything. I had her right through. I am thankful for her. (respondent 3)

The treatment of asylum-seeking women in hospitals whilst giving birth was mixed. Some reported that staff were too busy (respondents 16,11,7). Therefore, they were recipients of, instead of partners in their care, and their maternity experiences could be more like the National Service Frameworks standard. This may have been due to the demand for resources during the pandemic. Respondents often identified that the hospitals were not keeping women in, even when their baby was underweight, probably due to Covid.

Respondent 5 reported a very bad time in the hospital when she

perceived the nurse had just left her and never acted on her request for help.

This respondent had what she termed an accidental pregnancy with a boyfriend whom she has not seen since. She is hopeful the boyfriend returns to get her and the baby because she has no passport or visa to go to him *"My life is so bad there is no future"* (Respondent 5)

The findings from this data collection shed light on the challenges asylum-seeking mothers face during their maternity experiences, particularly in the hospital setting. Many of the issues raised by the participants, such as transient living situations, lack of partner support, and language barriers, were consistent with those identified in other recent reviews and inquiries into maternal and child health. The Confidential Enquiry into Maternal and Child Health (2007) highlighted the poorer outcomes for babies of minority women, which resonates with the experiences of asylum-seeking mothers in this study.

Hospital experiences for asylum-seeking mothers were a mixed bag. Some participants reported positive encounters with hospital staff who understood their unique circumstances and provided empathetic care. However, the experience was less satisfactory for others, with reports of being rushed through appointments and feeling like recipients rather than partners in their care.

The demand for resources during the pandemic may have contributed to this issue, leading to shorter hospital stays and limited support for some asylum-seeking mothers, even when their babies were underweight.

Language barriers and the sense of isolation were additional challenges faced by these women during their maternity care. Some participants reported needing someone who spoke their language in the health system, and they often found themselves navigating the process alone. However, a few fortunate asylum-seeking mothers found support from fellow patients, creating a sense of camaraderie during a vulnerable time.

One participant reported an incredibly distressing hospital experience, feeling neglected and unheard of by the nursing staff. Her situation was compounded by an accidental pregnancy with a boyfriend who had since disappeared, leaving her with no passport or visa to join him. This exemplifies the heightened vulnerability of asylum-seeking mothers, especially when facing unplanned pregnancies and lacking stable support systems.

In conclusion, the experiences of asylum-seeking mothers during their maternity journey are shaped by a complex interplay of challenges and support. While some aspects of hospital care were positive, there were also instances where the unique needs of these mothers were not adequately addressed. Addressing these disparities requires a comprehensive and compassionate approach from healthcare providers, considering the specific circumstances of asylum-seeking mothers and providing appropriate support and care throughout their pregnancy and childbirth. Ensuring asylum-seeking mothers access language support and culturally sensitive care can improve their maternity experiences and overall well-being. Policy changes and resource allocation should also be considered to address the disparities faced by vulnerable migrant populations, ultimately promoting better health outcomes for both mothers and their babies.

Breastfeeding

The subject of breastfeeding was not approached when asking the women about their birth, so the researcher asked an additional question about antenatal and breastfeeding lessons.

Most women in the refuge did not breastfeed, but some reported they had a lesson in the hospital about feeding.

In the U.K., I was sent to Derby; they detected I was pregnant, so they treated me as a pregnant lady who had to be accommodated. I had lessons in the hospital on breastfeeding. I left the hospital quickly. (respondent 8)

Breastfeeding was found difficult, and the mothers were not fully educated on how to get this started all the time. The lack of education may have resulted from a pandemic when clinic attendance was not a part of the services. At the refuge, very few out of 20 women breastfed. The others get the formula from charities or pay £6-£10 for each tin that lasts a week.

No one got any classes or help until Carriers of Hope came. (respondents 3,4,6,10.)

The women said no one talked about breastfeeding or birth once they were moved to the refuge; the refuge was in separate rooms with people keeping to themselves. *Until Carriers of Hope we all stayed in our room. Now we can meet for activities and singing.* (respondent 8)

It was also clear that women may not understand breastfeeding and its benefits. *I left the hospital within 24 hours. A breastfeeding lady called once. My baby doesn't want the breast -she is lazy.* (respondent 4)

Respondent 3 tried feeding but felt the poor food choice with her little money affected the baby's milk. She thought what she was eating was making bad milk.

I breastfed for six months, but she doesn't like the milk all the time crying, so I went to formula. I started the food for my baby at five months, just one time in the day. This respondent described a day where she was totally tied up with cooking for the baby weaning and feeding and having no time to herself.

Speaking for another woman who had newly arrived from the hotel and could not speak English, a respondent said, "*she could not breastfeed she had no food she is too thin.*" this resonates with other reports about pregnant women in the hotel. Tim Naor-Hilton, head of asylum at Refugee Action, reported his charity knew of several pregnant women currently in hotels, including a woman who gave birth recently. "*She's in the hotel with a new baby with no cash support, relying on these meals for nutrition, when she's just been discharged from hospital*", he wrote.

There is often stress about living with a tight budget and being unable to feed their baby. If they have a young child, they may get extra money on top of £35. The respondents described feeling tired out and unable to walk for their groceries, so even if they had the money for their food, the whole responsibility of the baby was on them whilst they were in the first weeks of refuge living.

Volunteers could be used to give the women a break at times to sleep or have a bath, just like an extended family would. Some charities have volunteers that speak various languages and could assist with this work.

The data on breastfeeding experiences among asylum-seeking mothers in the refuge highlights the challenges and barriers to initiating and sustaining breastfeeding. While some women received breastfeeding lessons during their hospital stay, many reported difficulties with breastfeeding and a lack of education on the subject.

One significant obstacle to breastfeeding was the lack of support and resources, particularly during the pandemic when clinic attendance was limited. As a result, very few women in the refuge breastfed their babies, and the majority relied on formula milk, either provided by charities or purchased at a considerable cost.

The importance of education and support in promoting breastfeeding was evident in the responses. Respondents expressed receiving classes or assistance only once Carriers of Hope stepped in, indicating a lack of awareness and guidance on breastfeeding techniques and benefits. This lack of information might have contributed to some women giving up on breastfeeding prematurely due to perceived challenges or misconceptions about their breast milk.

Moreover, the issue of inadequate nutrition and access to food emerged as a significant concern for breastfeeding mothers. Some respondents believed that their limited food choices, influenced by financial constraints, affected the quality of their breast milk, impacting their babies' feeding habits. This finding emphasises the importance of providing adequate nutrition and support to breastfeeding mothers to ensure the well-being of both mother and baby.

Additionally, the language barrier was another factor hindering the breastfeeding experiences of some asylum-seeking mothers. The inability to communicate effectively with healthcare professionals may have prevented them from seeking appropriate help or guidance on breastfeeding.

The data also shed light on the dire circumstances faced by pregnant women in hotels who lacked essential support and nutrition after giving birth. The reliance on hotel-provided meals for nutrition and the absence of cash support creates a distressing situation for these new mothers and their babies, highlighting the urgent need for comprehensive and compassionate support systems for pregnant asylum seekers.

In conclusion, the findings underscore the importance of providing accessible and culturally sensitive education and support on breastfeeding to asylum-seeking mothers. Improving access to antenatal and postnatal care and addressing the underlying challenges of nutrition and language barriers can significantly enhance breastfeeding rates and mothers' and babies' overall well-being. Additionally, adequate support and resources for pregnant women in hotels are essential to ensure they receive the necessary care and nutrition during this critical period. Policy changes and targeted interventions are crucial to addressing these issues and ensuring asylum-seeking mothers can make informed and empowered choices about breastfeeding and maternal health.

IN THEIR OWN WORDS

Multi-Agency Working

In most cases, asylum seekers were accessing maternity care later than is recommended and had fewer than the recommended number of antenatal appointments. The lack of care puts these women at increased risk of pregnancy-related complications

They treated me well in Birmingham in a hotel. I was pregnant there. There were no classes about giving birth -the doctor who saw me was not sure I was pregnant. We did blood tests to find out. Baby daddy is not involved, so I was on my own worried the baby was too small (respondent 6)

I still get care from a doctor but only to check the baby's weight. In Manchester, they checked my stitches. I thought I had to pay, but I did not. (respondent 17)

Some countries do not have developed multi-agency work, so this can be a surprise to the women. They sought medical help from the researcher and anyone else in their network, such as foodbank monitors. The women were surprised that the health visitors had contact with the charity and the other agencies. They were surprised that the state would intervene in child protection and others feared that their baby was at risk of being removed by someone. *When Carrying my baby, I was worried scared of losing her because of my past scared; they came to take my baby.* (respondent 4)

Some of the respondents were interested in the fact laws protected the child, and they have to report children in need. This also presented a fear that one would talk to the other and get them thrown out of the refuge or, worse, sent back. *I don't want to tell on her because it will get her thrown out, and I was like that with nowhere to stay.* (respondent 4)

For some, the journey to the refuge was helped by social workers and charity staff but during COVID-19 they never visited the refuge regularly.

I was different to the others. I had really good friends, and the medical staff rang me every day to see if I was ok. It was a domestic violence charity that got me moved. (respondent 12) The majority of women did not know about policy and guidelines changes, e.g., screening for domestic abuse in pregnancy. Some felt very unsafe because some women brought in men friends who continued to behave aggressively towards them and banged on other women's doors in the refuge.

This indicates information should be given about domestic violence and women's rights. Help lines should be on the wall in different languages.

There were mixed comments about health care availability, with the doctors being more unavailable than health visitors. The Coventry way is to register all asylum seekers with one practice, the Meridian, which operates in town -a bus ride away for these women.

Health visitors came to this refuge every two weeks, but we can call her; she is always here to help us, and we can get help. I knew about Covid information before I was pregnant and nurses were in town, so if I had the bus fare, I could attend maternity meetings and appointment with them. G.P. gave information about covid, and I read news from the phone. (respondent 4) . There are fears that the baby may be taken away from some women, and it is unclear how they know this.

Respondent 8 was worried because of her son *"my baby had ear pain, and G.P. did not help. He was always crying. Doctors are in town Meridiam practice. We can telephone only, so the baby wasn't checked."*

One respondent described getting a bus to the hospital because she was not feeling well and taking her 6-month-old son with her. They told her not to bring the baby into the hospital, so she got a bus back to the refuge and lay down feeling worse. The women do not know how to use the health systems and helplines. This added to her despondency about being alone with her son.

Other women had ongoing baby health worries *"Have you anything for his skin? He is poorly"* (respondent 15 asked the charity worker. It looked like eczema and dry skin problems had spread down the baby's chin to his arms.

The woman tried to help respondent nine, who had no English, to get medical help for her baby, but the doctors *"were always not there"*.

Some women have medication for depression but say they cannot use it because the baby is there. According to the women in the refuge, some women sleep for days due to medication, and most are used to babies crying for days. *"This woman was given medication for depression, so she does sleep a lot of night and day. I wonder if her baby is given drugs. He sleeps a lot."* (respondent 6)

The data from this section of the study reveals a concerning pattern of limited access to timely and comprehensive maternity care for asylum-seeking women. Many respondents accessed maternity care later than recommended and had fewer antenatal appointments than optimal. This lack of proper care puts these women at increased risk of pregnancy-related complications, underscoring the urgent need for improved healthcare services and support for this vulnerable population.

Language and cultural barriers were evident as obstacles in accessing healthcare for asylum-seeking women. Some respondents expressed surprise and confusion at the multi-agency approach to healthcare in the UK, seeking assistance from the researcher and foodbank monitors. Others feared intervention by child protection services, leading to reluctance to seek help for fear of potential repercussions, such as being thrown out of the refuge or facing deportation.

The data also highlights the importance of providing information about domestic violence, women's rights, and healthcare services available to asylum-seeking women. Information and helplines should be accessible in multiple languages to facilitate communication and support.

Mixed comments on the availability of healthcare services were reported, with some respondents facing challenges accessing doctors and relying more on health visitors. For asylum-seeking women, getting to the Meridian practice, which operates in town, maybe a significant logistical challenge, particularly for those in the refuge. This further emphasises the need to improve healthcare accessibility and provide better support for asylum-seeking women in their healthcare journeys.

Mental health concerns were also prevalent among the respondents, with some reporting depression and anxiety. However, there were difficulties in using medication for depression due to concerns about the impact on their babies and uncertainty about healthcare systems.

Overall, the findings from this data emphasise the urgent need for improved maternity care services for asylum-seeking women, including timely access to antenatal appointments, language and culturally sensitive healthcare support, and information on available resources. Enhancing support networks, providing clear information about healthcare options, and addressing mental health concerns can significantly improve asylum-seeking women's well-being and health outcomes during their maternity experiences. Policy changes and targeted interventions are essential to bridge the gaps in healthcare access and ensure the protection and well-being of asylum-seeking mothers and their babies.

The systems do not always help women. If they do not stay in the refuge there, the money will be stopped, but if they are vulnerable to men taking them in as "friend", they are vulnerable to being trafficked.

I left my country pregnant and came here for safety. I cannot eat the food they gave us, I can't get the food voucher; it is such a long walk. My baby is a very, very tiny boy, so I am going to stay with a friend. (respondent 7)

The interviews indicated the primary, tertiary and secondary health systems must be explained. Health services are limited basic child illness courses should be available, but this would take technology such as internet connections and computers.

Charities

In the hotel women have the financial support of £5.39 a day because they are provided with meals, leaving them unable to buy additional supplies such as toiletries and baby milk and cannot use public transport. In the refuge they pay for their food, but the nearest shops are Sainsbury, so the money doesn't go very far. The involvement of charities is vital to keep the women fed.

The need to learn how to cook English food and wean their child on something nutritious is clear. All of the women talked about the Carriers of Hope cooking project that gives appropriate cultural food, pots and woks and English cookery lessons. It also creates a legacy for the women inviting them to cook meals and post recipes onto their" what's ap" for others to share.

I think the shared activity is good for us. We all laugh and cook in the kitchen together. It helps us to forget things. (respondent 6)

IN THEIR OWN WORDS

I loved moving to the refuge and am thankful to charities that bring food. My baby eats potatoes now! (respondent, 17).

In Nigeria, those foods are expensive, and now the baby is also eating; he hates porridge; he finished it in the day, and it goes fast. Sainsbury is my nearest shop, and it is expensive; when I had a food voucher, it helped bring soup. (respondent 17)

When I moved to the refuge, I can't speak English, so COH helped me to get everything for the baby food, gloves and clothes. (respondent 3)

Women interviewed in this study highlighted several pockets of good practice. These occurred in services that had assistants or advocates and staff who demonstrated cross-cultural competence and compassion. For example, the charities St Francis send food parcels and supply baby items. Langer Aid brought food. Carriers of hope bring food and women's clothes, household items, clothes, and regular group teaching sessions.

Many women mentioned the same fact of being too poor to buy food *It is not easy because the money isn't enough for us and the baby. It is better now we have charities.* (respondent 1,3,4,5,10,12,17 and 18)

In this refuge Carriers of Hope were the first people to give us help. If I did not have the help, we had too little money. (respondent 10)

The charities Carriers of Hope came and brought nappies had enough food they treated me so nice. Then the Health visitor came. (respondent 17)

Without charities, I would be such broke milk nappies (respondent 4).

At this refuge, I was so hungry they were late with the Aspen card. The first people to help were St Francis, Joanna. Then a phone call from Wendu asylum help and he helped with weekly nappies, food and dresses fruit (respondent 1)

The Carriers of Hope did lessons on Covid and brought in a scanner to keep checking everyone's temperature, and It felt safer for my baby (respondent 6).

I learnt about safe sleeping and weaning and my babies development (respondent 4)

Without charities and food banks, these women would be as badly off for nutritious food as other community asylum seekers. In this respect, they are different from other research participants when looking at food poverty.

Refuge living

The women reported a mixture of pros and cons of living in a refuge

It fun being here the mixture is Africans and Albanians (respondent 15). *There is everything we need* (respondent 17). *Waiting to get settled into our own home.* (respondent 1) another respondent, 6, talked about how other women helped her. *When I gave birth, I had food, but the other ladies did not help until they found I had caesareans so that i couldn't move. They cooked for me.*

I have help in the house if I want to wash, my friends will help and hold my baby, but we don't sleep; The babies all cry at different times. (respondent 6)

The majority reported it was right when they all got together to cook -a project from a charity, Carriers of Hope. *We laugh and talk deep with each other altogether, the Africans and the Albanians and the Chinese* (respondent 18) many reported finding a friend there. *Women in the house are good to me Blessing, and I moved in, and we helped each other. My baby had constipation, and she helped me. We called the hospital for an emergency. respondent six and respondent 17 are my friends.* (Respondent 10)

The data from this set underscores the critical role of charities and support organisations in meeting the essential needs of asylum-seeking women during their maternity experiences. In hotels and the refuge, financial constraints and limited resources left these women struggling to access necessities, such as food, toiletries, and baby supplies. The support provided by charities, such as St Francis, Langer Aid, and Carriers of Hope, has been instrumental in addressing these challenges and ensuring that the women and their babies receive the care and assistance they require.

In the refuge, the involvement of Carriers of Hope has been particularly impactful. Their cooking project provides culturally appropriate food and cookery lessons and fosters a sense of community and camaraderie among the women. The shared activities and support offered by the charity have been vital in helping these women overcome the hardships they face and find joy and support in their shared experiences.

The data also highlights pockets of good practice in certain services that demonstrate cross-cultural competence and compassion. These services, equipped with assistants or advocates, have supported asylum-seeking women during their maternity journey.

The importance of charities in providing crucial resources and support cannot be overstated. Respondents consistently mentioned the significant impact of organisations like Carriers of Hope, St Francis, and others in meeting their needs for food, baby items, and assistance. Many of these women would be even more vulnerable to food poverty and financial hardship without such support.

Moreover, the support provided by these charities extends beyond material assistance. Carriers of Hope, for example, offers essential lessons on topics such as safe sleeping, weaning, and babies' development, enhancing the mothers' knowledge and confidence in caring for their infants.

In conclusion, the data highlights the indispensable role of charities and support organisations in ensuring the well-being and survival of asylum-seeking women and their babies during pregnancy and childbirth. The support provided goes beyond material assistance, fostering community and empowerment among these women. To address the challenges asylum-seeking women face, continued investment in support services, cross-cultural training for healthcare professionals, and access to essential resources are essential. Policy changes and increased collaboration between agencies and charities can significantly improve the maternity experiences and well-being of asylum-seeking women, allowing them to navigate this critical phase of their lives with dignity and support.

However, for some refuge, living is unbearable. The theme is there are no people to make the refuge rules, so the strongest characters that can shout the loudest will remain the rule-makers.

Refuge living has difficulties; too many people misunderstand that ladies fight for stupid things food goes missing. The toilet is shared and not cleaned. (respondent 18)

When there are good people around you its ok but bullying and fighting goes on (respondent 4)

I don't feel safe here. They don't like to share with anyone else. They have such a lot of clothes, so they grab more. They can buy them or find cheap clothes. (respondent 2)

They are so greedy they take everything and stack up their room. There is no place for the baby to play in their room. (respondent 13)

I hate them at times I hide (respondent 4). This lack of safety in the refuge is supported by many residents who report trying to separate themselves from chaotic pushing when the food or clothes arrive. The sharing of kitchen utensils and fridge space also incites confrontations.

The sharing and group living is stressful, and most women say 20 sharing the house is too many. There are plenty of clothes going in weekly from Carriers of Hope. The reality and anxiety that they will have their room searched by other women and robbed was talked about by the women. *The house is very tiny; we have 20 people!!!.* (respondent 16)

We act like animals grabbing things and fighting like I don't feel safe I want to move (respondent 13)

Other problems that the women talked about at length are that the repairs of property they live in. SERCO is the landlord and might also be the refuge owner.

The rooms are tiny and some leak on the clothes. During my pregnancy, I had to buy more than one mattress; the beds are very uncomfortable and give you back pain. (respondent 4)

The baby wants to sleep with the mothers, and I sleep in the end. I asked for a double bed from Carriers Of Hope, but it doesn't come. I have two mattresses; you can't sleep in those beds. (respondent 4 and 18)

Respondents also identified feeling very low in the mood *I miss my life* (respondent 5).

I am just waiting, and nothing happens; my solicitor doesn't do anything; I just keep ringing them (respondent 10).

Most respondents said they had no family here, and they often said something about their baby keeping them from ending their life.

I want to cry but manage myself because of my baby. (respondent 13) Most reported that not knowing how long they are in the refuge is a constant downer on their life.

It is not good in the house because of the noise all the babies cry at once (respondent 3, 8 and 11); respondent 11 has severe mental health difficulties, and others in the house say they are scared of her *"going off".*

Group living was a chosen topic of conversation for all of the respondents with good and bad points being made.

The refuge is so hard to stay here all the time.
I stay because I am safe for me and my baby.
The house is not just one or two; it has too many girls.
The room is so small for one-year baby she can't walk.
The bed is small; the baby cannot walk.
I am feeling good to be there, but some women are fighting and loud the too many different people from different countries. Different food. I don't want to say something wrong, but they don't understand my English

In conclusion, there are positives and negatives to refuge living, as respondent 17 said *In the refuge, it's good enjoying living with my baby. In the refuge, there are so many babies, and we meet in the lounge to play with other babies meeting different people from different places, learning about new places and sharing ideas. On the other hand, we have issues we are not equal; we came from different places, and the others are so different characters their nationality makes them behave differently.*

Dreams and Hopes

Some of the respondents know this is just a stopping point until the baby is one year old, and they think they will be given their own house to live in. Many wanted to start training and work in care.

Hoping to get settled, and my baby will go to school. (respondent 18)

After the refuge, I am planning to apply for NVQ this September, go to school and being at work in health care. I have a passion for caring for people. Work with the NHS. I will get my papers and be able to work; to care for people. (respondent 17)

(respondent 3) *Starting my life with my baby, I want to learn English and start college.*

Dreams my baby healthy a happy child, my case to be resolved to get a visa to work here to have my own family my own life. I can't wait for the Home Office to make a decision. I don't want people every time to help me. I am not a parasite. (respondent 4)

I just want a visa just live here. I feel safe in the UK. (respondent 8). *I have been waiting for over one year; my fiancé is in another country with a job. `he can claim the baby, and I hope to be claimed and move there too. I am so tired and lonely* (respondent 5),

Many of the women yearned for family members and another way of living. *Hoping My husband will be here with me. Sera leone is too dangerous to go back.* (respondent 6)

at home, we would have a big party for the baby. my mother doesn't know I have a baby (respondent 8)

I can never go back. My dad is against my relationship with the wrong boy. It is a hard, long story to tell. Not easy to be in a country where you don't have a family. If I go back, my dad will kill me (respondent 1).

I want to be someone who can help people by translating. (respondent 4)

Many were stifled by living in the refuge with so many others and yearned for privacy and their own home

I Hope for a better life than this one to live on my own leave me and my child alone. (respondent 17)

I wish the Home office would just grant me residence (respondent 13)

I hope my big wish to get my papers to go back to school to study for nursing (respondent 5)

Previous research on maternity services and complex social factors led to NICE (2010) issuing guidelines for women in need. However, this study reveals that the communication between women and relevant agencies still needs to be improved even after ten years, resulting in unmet emotional needs during their baby's first year. This case study identifies security and mental health needs among asylum-seeking women. It highlights the necessity for support workers to engage in group work within the refuge to promote mental well-being. However, such assistance was lacking within the refuge, leading to challenges accessing mental health services online due to limited phones, data, and language barriers. Asylum seekers aspire to build family lives and work in the UK. Unfortunately, research indicates that the processing time for asylum claims is much longer than the government websites claim, causing further uncertainty and stress for these individuals.

Regarding general baby health, the study found that the babies' needs, such as play and breastfeeding, were not consistently met. Breastfeeding rates were low, with only a few out of 20 babies receiving breast milk. The cost of tongue-tie procedures posed financial barriers, forcing mothers to resort to bottle-feeding. Instances of inadequate healthcare were reported, such as an accident involving a burnt baby without access to medical care, eczema and allergies resulting from poor food advice, and difficulties reaching a GP for constipation or other health concerns. A child's introductory health lesson booklet, commonly given to new mothers, was not received by any of the women, highlighting a lack of information during their hospital stay. Digital poverty and the lack of broadband further exacerbate the information gap. As babies grow older, they can be seen as nuisances requiring more attention, leading some women to discipline them for normal development. Discussion of child ages and stages, as well as modelling playtime to stimulate babies, is necessary. Lack of access to toys, post-traumatic stress, and postnatal depression in mothers often hindered play interactions. The study reveals poor attitudes towards asylum-seeking women during hospital visits, corroborating previous research on the adverse treatment experienced by migrant women. Improved education and awareness among maternity workers, charity workers, and other relevant parties about the local situation is necessary.

Additionally, additional support is needed for mental health needs, domestic abuse, and young asylum-seeking women who are pregnant or new parents. Communication between different levels of healthcare services, including statutory health, social, immigration services, and the voluntary sector, is severely lacking when caring for vulnerable and migrant populations. Insufficient communication between charities and community midwifery staff can lead to duplication and resource waste. Limited engagement with community-based support services further compounds the burden on women, mainly due to COVID-19-related disruptions. Difficulties arise for women who cannot give birth in a stable environment with familiar people and face challenges accessing transportation for appointments. Obtaining information in their language, especially regarding services and specific health needs such as diabetes during childbirth, proves problematic. COVID-19 restrictions have also resulted in the absence of antenatal and postnatal classes and limited visits from health visitors to women in the refuge. The birth experience is often disempowering for asylum-seeking women due to hostility, racism, and a lack of autonomy in decision-making. After birth, women are left to return to the hostel, and many experience symptoms of postnatal depression or post-traumatic stress, exacerbated by isolation and unmet needs. Listening to women's stories is vital to creating awareness among local services about the specific care required for asylum seekers. Effective collaboration between charities and statutory services requires regular meetings and discussions to overcome divisions and hierarchies. By working together, different services such as domestic violence agencies, social care, migrant support, and charities can support and settle new mothers emotionally and financially.

19 LAST WORD

Upon nearing the conclusion of my book, I feel a profound sense of achievement. My literary voyage has revolved around a thorough investigation of the intricate interplay between academic theory and its practical application in educational writing. As I delved deeper into this subject, the symbiotic relationship between theory and practice became increasingly apparent—two forces deeply entwined, influencing and shaping each other.

The ardent pursuit of knowledge led me to recognise that academic writing serves as a potent bridge, effectively connecting theory with practice. Through critical engagement with academic theories and their active application, writing has the capacity to generate novel insights, challenge established perspectives, and foster intellectual progress. In essence, academic writing transcends a mere reflection of ideas, assuming the role of a medium that fosters innovation and advancement.

In the seclusion of my study, I engaged in profound introspection of the transformative journey I undertook. Witnessing the seamless flow between ideas and their practical manifestation, my writing assumed the role of a catalyst for change—an avenue for discourse that invited critique, expansion, and engagement from others.

Upon penning the final sentences of my book, my vision for the future encompasses a world where the demarcation between theory and practice continues to blur, and academic writing garners recognition as a potent tool for translating abstract ideas into tangible realities.

While humbly acknowledging that my contribution is a modest one in the vast realm of academic writing, it stands as a testament to the potential of this craft to shape the landscape of knowledge. Through my words, I become part of a lineage of thinkers and writers united by our shared pursuit of knowledge and unwavering commitment to pushing the boundaries of human understanding. I take solace in the knowledge that my words will reach the hands and minds of fellow scholars and practitioners, inspiring them to embark on their explorations, intertwine theory and practice, and forge new pathways in the domain of academic writing.

As the book draws to a close, it is important to recognise that the narratives of refugee women persist and extend beyond the confines of its pages. The stories and experiences captured within these chapters are not confined to the literary realm but are lived realities for these courageous women. Their journeys, struggles, and triumphs endure, shaping their lives and influencing the communities they belong to. While the book may conclude, the indomitable spirit of these refugee women persists, reminding us of the ongoing importance of understanding, supporting, and advocating for their resilience and well-being in the face of adversity.

REFERENCES

A

Abd Samad, A., Eng, W.B., Arshad, N.I. and Kalpany, K., 2016, November. Accuracy of English Pronoun Use among Malaysian Esl 5-6 Year Old Children and Teaching Implications in the Malaysian Pre-School Education Context. In 3rd International Conference on Early Childhood Education (ICECE 2016) (pp. 84-90). Atlantis Press.

Ager, A., and A. Strang. 2008. "Understanding Integration: A Conceptual Framework." Journal of Refugee Studies 21 (2): 166–191. doi:10.1093/jrs/fen016.

Al-Ramahi, M., Shakibazadeh, E., Atashzadeh-Shoorideh, F., and Moslemirad, M. 2018. Barriers to healthcare access for refugees with disabilities in Iran: A qualitative study. BMC international health and human rights, 18(1), 23.

Andrew, A., Cattan, S., Dias, M.C., Farquharson, C., Kraftman, L., Krutikova, S., Phimister, A. and Sevilla, A., 2020. Family time use and home learning during the COVID-19 lockdown(No. R178). IFS Report.

Ashworth, P., Bannister, P., Thorne, P. and Students on the Qualitative Research Methods Course Unit, 1997. Guilty in whose eyes? University students' perceptions of cheating and plagiarism in academic work and assessment. Studies in higher education, 22(2), pp.187-203.

Atlas, S., 2023. ChatGPT for higher education and professional development: A guide to conversational AI

B

Bajwa, J., S. Couto, S. Kidd, R. Markoulakis, M. Abai, and K. McKenzie. 2017. "Refugees, Higher Education, and Informational Barriers." Refuge: Canada's Journal on Refugees 33 (2): 56–65. doi:10.7202/1043063ar.

Baker, S., 2018. Shifts in the treatment of knowledge in academic reading and writing: Adding complexity to students' transitions between A-levels and university in the UK. Arts and Humanities in Higher Education, 17(4), pp.388-409.

Baker, S., G. Ramsay, E. Irwin, and L. Miles. 2018a. "'Hot', 'Cold' and 'Warm' Supports: Towards Theorising Where Refugee Students Go for Assistance at University." Teaching in Higher Education 23 (1): 1–16.

Banihashem, S.K., Noroozi, O. and Wals, A., 2023. A SWOT analysis of ChatGPT: Implications for educational practice and research. Innovations in Education and Teaching International, pp.1-15.

Bauloz, C., Vathi, Z. and Acosta, D., 2019. Migration, inclusion and social cohesion: Challenges, recent developments and opportunities. World Migration Report 2020, pp.186-206.

Bauloz, C., Z. Vathi, and D. Acosta. 2019. "Migration, Inclusion and Social Cohesion: Challenges, Recent Developments and Opportunities." In World Migration Report 2020. United Nations. doi:10.18356/0095ab48-en.

Bayrakdar, S. and Guveli, A., 2020. Inequalities in home learning and schools' provision of distance teaching during school closure of COVID-19 lockdown in the UK (No. 2020-09). ISER Working Paper Series.

Becker, C., & Roos, J. 2016. An approach to creative speaking activities in the young learners' classroom. Education Inquiry, 7(1),

Black, P., Harrison, C., Lee, C., Marshall, B. and Wiliam, D., 2004. Working inside the black box: Assessment for learning in the classroom. Phi delta kappan, 86(1), pp.8-21.

Bloch, A., 2008. Refugees in the UK labour market: The conflict between economic integration and policy-led labour market restriction. Journal of Social Policy, 37(1), pp.21-36.

Borwick, S., Schweitzer, R.D., Brough, M., Vromans, L. and Shakespeare-Finch, J., 2013. Well-being of refugees from Burma: A salutogenic perspective. International Migration, 51(5), pp.91-105.

Brabazon, T., 2015. Turnitin? Turn it off: The deskilling of information literacy. Turkish Online Journal of Distance Education, 16(3).

Brabazon, T., 2002. Digital hemlock: Internet education and the poisoning of teaching. UNSW Press.

Bradby, H., Humphris, R., and Padilla, B. 2015. Fertility, pregnancy, and childbirth: refugee women's experiences in resettlement. Journal of reproductive and infant psychology, 33(4), 422-433.

C

Castro, F.G. and Murray, K.E., 2010. Cultural adaptation and resilience. Handbook of adult resilience, pp.375-403.

Caul, S., 2021. Deaths registered weekly in England and Wales, provisional: week ending 5th Nov J 2021. found at https://www.ons.gov.uk/peoplepopulationandcommunity/birthsdeathsandmarriages/deaths/bulletins/deathsregisteredweeklyinenglandandwalesprovisional/5november2021

Chen, S., Chen, C. and Wen, P., 2021. Parental anxiety, endorsement of literacy learning, and home literacy practices among Chinese parents of young children. Reading and Writing, pp.1-28.

Chomsky, N., 2000. The architecture of language.

Cocks, T. and Stokes, J., 2013. Policy into practice: A case study of widening participation in Australian higher education. Widening Participation and Lifelong Learning, 15(1), pp.22-38.

D

Dankova, P. and Giner, C., 2011. Technology in aid of learning for isolated refugees. Forced Migration Review, (38), p.11.

Dingle, G.A., Sharman, L.S., Bauer, Z., Beckman, E., Broughton, M., Bunzli, E., Davidson, R., Draper, G., Fairley, S., Farrell, C. and Flynn, L.M., 2021. How do music activities affect health and well-being? A scoping review of studies examining psychosocial mechanisms. Frontiers in Psychology, p.3689.

Dong, Y.R., 1996. Learning how to use citations for knowledge transformation: Non-native doctoral students' dissertation writing in science. Research in the Teaching of English, pp.428-457.

Dwivedi, Y.K., Kshetri, N., Hughes, L., Slade, E.L., Jeyaraj, A., Kar, A.K., Baabdullah, A.M., Koohang, A., Raghavan, V., Ahuja, M. and Albanna, H., 2023. "So what if ChatGPT wrote it?" Multidisciplinary perspectives on opportunities, challenges and implications of generative conversational AI for research, practice and policy. International Journal of Information Management, 71, p.102642.

E

Earnest, J., Joyce, A., De Mori, G. and Silvagni, G., 2010. Are universities responding to the needs of students from refugee backgrounds?. Australian Journal of Education, 54(2), pp.155-174.

Ethics: Using ChatGPT for research may raise ethical concerns, particularly around privacy and data security. Tlili, A., Shehata, B., Adarkwah, M.A., Bozkurt, A., Hickey, D.T., Huang, R. and Agyemang, B., 2023. What if the devil is my guardian angel: ChatGPT as a case study of using chatbots in education. Smart Learning Environments, 10(1), p.15.

Esser, H., 2006. Migration, language and integration. Berlin: WZB.

F

Fassler, R., 1998. Room for talk: Peer support for getting into English in an ESL kindergarten. Early Childhood Research Quarterly, 13(3), pp.379-409.

Felder and Henriques 1995 Felder, R.M. and Henriques, E.R., 1995. Learning and teaching styles in foreign and second language education. Foreign language annals, 28(1), pp.21-31.

Ferguson, N., Laydon, D., Nedjati Gilani, G., Imai, N., Ainslie, K., Baguelin, M., Bhatia, S., Boonyasiri, A., Cucunuba Perez, Z.U.L.M.A., Cuomo-Dannenburg, G. and Dighe, A., 2020. Report 9: Impact of non-pharmaceutical interventions (NPIs) to reduce COVID-19 mortality and healthcare demand.

Frimberger, K., 2016. Towards a well-being focussed language pedagogy: enabling arts-based, multilingual learning spaces for young people with refugee backgrounds. Pedagogy, Culture & Society, 24(2), pp.285-299.

G

Gudmundsdottir, H.R. and Gudmundsdottir, D.G., 2010. Parent–infant music courses in Iceland: perceived benefits and mental well-being of mothers. Music Education Research, 12(3), pp.299-309.

H

Harrell-Bond, B. E., & Voutira, E. 1992. Anthropology and the Study of Refugees. Anthropology Today, 8(4), 6. https://doi.org/10.2307/2783530

Hedges, H., Cullen, J. and Jordan, B., 2011. Early years curriculum: Funds of knowledge as a conceptual framework for children's interests. Journal of Curriculum Studies, 43(2), pp.185-205.

Higginbottom, G.M., Safipour, J., Yohani, S., O'Brien, B., Mumtaz, Z., Paton, P., Chiu, Y. and Barolia, R., 2016. An ethnographic investigation of the maternity healthcare experience of immigrants in rural and urban Alberta, Canada. BMC pregnancy and childbirth, 16(1), pp.1-15.

Hinshaw, T., Clift, S., Hulbert, S. and Camic, P.M., 2015. Group singing and young people's psychological well-being. International Journal of Mental Health Promotion, 17(1), pp.46-63.

Holt, L. and Murray, L., 2022. Children and Covid 19 in the UK. Children's Geographies, 20(4), pp.487-494.

Hsieh, M.F. and Teo, T., 2021. Examining early childhood teachers' perspectives of collaborative teaching with English language teachers. English Teaching & Learning, pp.1-20.

I

J

K

Kennedy, M.S., Newland, J.A. and Owens, J.K., 2017. Findings from the INANE survey on student papers submitted to nursing journals. Journal of Professional Nursing, 33(3), pp.175-183.

Klein, J. B., Jacobs R. H., and Reinecke M. A. 2007. "Cognitive-behavioral Therapy for Adolescent Depression: A Meta-Analytic Investigation of Changes in Effect-size Estimates." Journal of the American Academy of Child & Adolescent Psychiatry 46 (11): 1403–1413

L

Lo, Y.C., Goswami, J.S. and Inoue, K., 2009. Attitudes of pre-service teachers toward English language learners. In Asian EFL Journal Cebu Conference, Cebu Philippines.

M

McBrien, J.L., 2005. Educational needs and barriers for refugee students in the United States: A review of the literature. Review of educational research, 75(3), pp.329-364.

Moher, D., Liberati, A., Tetzlaff, J., Altman, D.G. and PRISMA Group*, 2009. Preferred reporting items for systematic reviews and meta-analyses: the PRISMA statement. Annals of internal medicine, 151(4), pp.264-269.

Moher, David, Alessandro Liberati, Jennifer Tetzlaff, Douglas G. Altman, and Prisma Group. 2009. "Preferred Reporting Items for Systematic Reviews and Meta-Analyses: The PRISMA Statement." PLoS Med 6 (7): e1000097.

Miettinen, R., 2000. The concept of experiential learning and John Dewey's theory of reflective thought and action. International journal of lifelong education, 19(1), pp.54-72.

Mudzielwana, N.P., 2016. The conceptualisation of Language and Vocabulary Learning Strategies: Key Aspect in Every Curriculum Area. International Journal of Educational Sciences, 15(3), pp.538-546.

N

O

Obeid, R. and Hill, D.B., 2017. An intervention designed to reduce plagiarism in a research methods classroom. Teaching of Psychology, 44(2), pp.155-159.

P

Phillimore, J. and Goodson, L., 2008. Making a place in the global city: The relevance of indicators of integration. Journal of Refugee Studies, 21(3), pp.305-325.

Pinker, S., 1995. Language acquisition. Language: An invitation to cognitive science, 1, pp.135-82.

Q
R
S

Sheikh, M. and Anderson, J.R., 2018. Acculturation patterns and education of refugees and asylum seekers: A systematic literature review. Learning and Individual Differences, 67, pp.22-32.

Snyder, N. 2019. Matter Of A-b-, Lgbtq Asylum Claims, And The Rule Of Law In The U.S. Asylum System. Northwestern University Law Review, 114(3), 809.olii

Sommer, T.E., Gomez, C.J., Yoshikawa, H., Sabol, T., Chor, E., Sanchez, A., Chase-Lansdale, P.L. and Brooks-Gunn, J., 2020. Head Start, two-generation ESL services, and parent engagement. Early Childhood Research Quarterly, 52, pp.63-73.

Stewart, H., Watson, N. and Campbell, M., 2018. The cost of school holidays for children from low-income families. Childhood, 25(4), pp.516-529.

Stuckler , D . Professor David Stuckler Click the link to apply for a free 1-to-1 accelerator session: https://www.stucklerconsulting.com/

T

Temple, B. and Moran, R. eds., 2006. Doing research with refugees: Issues and guidelines. Policy Press.T

U

United Nations High Commissioner for Refugees (UNHCR). State of the world's refugees. Oxford and New York: Oxford University Press.

United Nations High Commissioner for Refugees (UNHCR figures at a glance Geneva 2017 Available at https://www.unhcr.org/en-au/figures-at-a-glance.html accessed on 1/11/2021

Usher, K., Durkin, J. and Bhullar, N., 2020. The COVID-19 pandemic and mental health impacts. International Journal of Mental Health Nursing, 29(3), p.315.

V

Van Staden, A., 2018. HOPE VERSUS DESPONDENCY: EXPLORING THE LITERACY PROSPECTS OF SOUTH AFRICAN EARLY CHILDHOOD LEARNERS. In INTED2018 Proceedings (pp. 9175-9180). IATED.

Van Rhyn, A. and van Staden, A., 2018. Interactive storybook reading as an intervention strategy to support esl learners' reading comprehension. In Edulearn 18. 10th International Conference on Education and New Learning Technology:(Palma, 2nd-4th of July, 2018). Conference proceedings (pp. 10182-10186). IATED Academy.

Van Rhyn, A.A., 2018. Literacy development and self-concept of English second language learners: an exploratory study(Doctoral dissertation, University of the Free State).

Verdugo, D., & Belmonte, I. 2007. Using digital stories to improve listening compre- hension with Spanish young learners of English. Language Learning & Technology, 11(1), 87–101. Retrieved from http://llt.msu.edu/vol11num1/ramirez/